THEY STARTED TALKING

Frank Tuttle, an early publicity photograph.

THEY STARTED TALKING

by

Frank Tuttle

Edited, and with an Introduction,
by John Franceschina

BearManor Media
2005

They Started Talking
© 2005 The Frank Tuttle Estate
Introduction © 2005 John Franceschina
All rights reserved.

For information, address:

BearManor Media
P. O. Box 750
Boalsburg, PA 16827

bearmanormedia.com

Cover design by John Teehan

Typesetting and layout by John Teehan

Published in the USA by BearManor Media

Library of Congress Cataloging-in-Publication Data

Tuttle, Frank, 1892-1963.
They started talking / by Frank Tuttle ; edited, and with an introduction, by John Franceschina.
p. cm.
Includes index.
ISBN 1-59393-027-5

1. Tuttle, Frank, 1892-1963. 2. Motion picture producers and directors--United States--Biography. I. Franceschina, John Charles, 1947- II. Title.

PN1998.3.T89A3 2005
791.4302'3'092--dc22
2004029093

ISBN—1-59393-027-5

TABLE OF CONTENTS

Introduction i

They Started Talking 1

The Films of Frank Tuttle 201

Unpublished Stories and Essays 207

Unpublished Scenarios and Treatments 209

Unpublished Plays 211

Unpublished Screenplays and Adaptations 213

Writing on the Dance 215

Index 219

INTRODUCTION

Readers accustomed to tell-all autobiographies full of juicy innuendos and polemical disputations about religion, politics, and the price of gasoline, might be surprised at the outset with Frank Tuttle's autobiography, *They Started Talking*, a book designed to be more about making movies than about his political or personal life.

Best known as the director of *This Gun for Hire* and *Roman Scandals*, the name Frank Wright Tuttle perhaps has greater political than artistic resonance to those who recognize it today because of his association with the American Communist Party from 1937 to 1947 and his subsequent appearance before the House Committee on Un-American Activities. The climate surrounding the hearings in the 1940s and 50s tended to be reductive, defining and judging artists by their politics rather than their talent and creativity, and anyone who "named names" often became identified with that act rather than a significant body of artistic achievement. On 24 May 1951, Tuttle gave testimony, fully conscious of the effects it might have on his career, but convinced of the necessity of speaking out.

In a statement that anticipated by fifty years the political atmosphere in the war on terrorism, Tuttle argued: "I believe that there is a traditional dislike among Americans for informers, and I am an informer, and I have thought about this constantly. I believe all decent people who share this dislike for informers, if they think about this carefully, will agree with me that at this particular moment it is absolutely vital. In a case like this, with ruthless aggression abroad in the world, the aggressors, I believe, are as ruthless with their own people as they are with those they consider their enemies; and I feel that today it is absolutely necessary for Americans to be equally ruthless."

About his own political beliefs, Tuttle testified:

> I was a Communist during the fight against Nazism and Fascism. The Communists as a legal political party had written into their record that they would expel anyone who advocated the overthrow of the Government by force and violence. When the world political situation changed, I left the party and today I completely oppose its aims and tactics.
>
> I am sure you will understand that only the absolute truth about myself offers me any comfort today. I have thought constantly about every action of mine during my membership in the past. I submit, with all humility, that I can find nothing in anything I did or thought that was worse than a monstrous error in judgment as to the method I chose to promote peace and security and the well-being of my fellow men.

It is not surprising then that Tuttle's autobiographical manuscript is silent regarding his changing political biases except where it connects with his work. The only mention made of Communism in the book accompanies a reference to an anti-Communist 1955-56 television series, *Crusader*, some episodes of which he directed. As the author suggested in his introductory note, the focus of the book is on his film work and only those people and incidents that have been associated with that endeavor.[1]

Also unusual is the absence of personal details—the typical accounts of marriages, romances, children, and health issues—so often characteristic of artists' memoirs. Clearly, Frank Tuttle's private life did not encroach upon his professional career as a movie maker. However, to clarify the family pictures that appear as illustrations throughout the text, it is helpful to know that Frank was married three times: first to Fredericka Staats (with whom he had two children: Fredrika and Helen); next to Tatiana ("Tania") Smirnova (with whom he had one child, Barbara); and, finally, to Carla Boehm. Also, in a letter to Larry Adler, the harmonica virtuoso and composer, dated 28 March 1962, Tuttle notes that he has four grandsons, the oldest of which is fifteen.

Twenty years earlier, in 1942, *Hollywood Parade* described a Holly-

---

1. Even the FBI Files dealing with Tuttle's politics emphasized the importance of his work as a film director and teacher. One source (30-B-1) noted that in the 1920s Tuttle was rated in the same class as Cecil B. De Mille in the motion picture industry and concluded that "Tuttle's importance as a Communist comes from the fact, first, that he is recognized as a very capable motion picture director and, moreover, he is considered to be an excellent teacher of motion picture methods."

Introduction iii

wood party thrown by Frank and Tania Tuttle (to celebrate daughter Helen's arrival on the West Coast) that would have fit appropriately in one or another screwball comedy of the period:

> Having yielded to the persuasive pressure of feminine arts and wiles or the masculine force of patriotic argument, this morning finds many a Hollywood hotel clerk without the rubber counter mat upon which he had been wont to make change, also several filmland café proprietors looking wistfully at the entrance spot that was once marked by a rubber door mat upon which a thousand celebrated feet had trod.
> And with the smug smile of the cat that knew darn right well where the canary went, Frank and Tania Tuttle pulled up to their favorite gas station on the last day of the rubber drive with a veritable argosy of the precious loot in tow.
> You see, Frank's fair daughter, Helen, had just arrived from New York for a summer holiday in Hollywood, and it was the final day of the rubber drive, so in Helen's honor the Paramount director and his engaging spouse tossed a cocktail and buffet supper party at their Hollywoodland home, followed by a two-hour scavenger hunt and a midnight roundup at the Players.
> Well, the Robert Prestons won a book of war stamps for the most rubber collected; the Mischa Auers, who arrived with a huge rubber plant, were awarded a book for the funniest, and another prize went to Veronica Lake for the ingenuity and arduous effort she gave in collecting the greatly sought commodity.
> Other high pressured scavengers were Sue Carol (sic) and Alan Ladd.

Celebrities crowded Tuttle's life on and off camera, and it is no surprise that, in *They Started Talking*, the stories surrounding the making of movies managed to push the extraneous private familial anecdotes off the page.

Tuttle's reminiscences of his development as a playwright, initially as a student at Yale and subsequently as a writer-director for Paramount, introduce to the public this generally unknown facet of Tuttle's work. Of particular note are discussions of his early plays *Quentin Durward*, *Saint Bartholomew's Eve*, and *The Village*, and later film adaptations, notably *The Apple Tree*, from a story by John Galsworthy and various plays by George Bernard Shaw. Tuttle's daughter, Helen, recalled that he even planned to do a screen adaptation of Shakespeare's *Hamlet*.

Among Tuttle's original works that are not mentioned in his autobiography is a musical collaboration, first with Duke Ellington and later with Larry Adler, called *Free As a Bird*, which occupied Tuttle from the 1940s until his death. A "Musical Mirage" about an exotic princess who falls in love with a Christian missionary, the work offers an incisive indictment of slavery and a positive, unsanctimonious approach to religion—certainly a unique work for Tuttle who was not known to be a religious man.[2] Although Tuttle chose not to cite this work in his autobiography, I offer the following poetical extracts as evidence of the author's development as a lyricist—if only to invite comparison with those lyrics he quotes in his book.

Early in the first scene, Hushabeide, the Sultan's ex-favorite, teaches the harem girls their duties as wives:

> For a dutiful wife
> Must be a beautiful wife
> When her lord and master's returning.
> Though he's weary and lame,
> She must kindle a flame,
> Just to keep the home fires burning.
>
> With a metrical line,
> And a jugful of wine,
> 'Neath the bough of the pine
> Or the sago,
> Lead him on with your lips,
> With your eyes and your hips,
> And a total eclipse
> Of your ego.

---

2. Tuttle's daughter, Helen, recalled that she and her sister, Fredrika, went out to California to be with him following his heart attack: "He had always been an atheist so we were surprised when we asked him how he was feeling that he replied with lines from 'The Green Pastures,' 'I's fine Lawd, jest fine.'"

> Yes, a dutiful wife,
> Must be a beautiful wife,
> As she greets her master and pets him.
> But she'll never impart
> What is locked in her heart,
> For her lord only knows what she lets him.

Later in the same scene, Gham Al Duna, Sultan of Kapul Bash, expresses the world-weariness so often associated with money and power:

> I'm awake,
> But I ache
> At the prospect before me.
> I'm unfurl'd
> To a world
> Whose attractions all bore me.
> I emerge with an urge
> To kick over the traces;
> But what do I spot?
> The same old faces.
>
> There's nothing new beneath the sun,
> Nor underneath the moon.
> The jokes are few—the tales they've spun—
> I guess the point too soon.
> You find a new zip in the wine you sip.
> It's just the moustache on your upper lip.
> Compose a new tune—la re mi do—
> But Mozart wrote it—and years ago!
> Some blonde attracts you—divinely fair—
> She's last year's wife with this year's hair.
> Oh, itch to scratch and scratch to itch.
> That's sex they say, but what is which?
> There's nothing new beneath the sun,
> Nor underneath the moon.
> There's nothing due, I wouldn't shun,
> Except to sleep, till noon.

Even if some of the jokes fall flat after forty years, the author's sophisticated prosody manages to hold its own.

They Started Talking was written by Frank Wright Tuttle between 1960 and 1962. The manuscript is complete except for page 30 which, I suspect, chronicled the creation of the Film Guild, the substance of which I have attempted to reconstruct from contemporary newspaper accounts. But for the regularization of spelling and punctuation, the rest of the book appears here exactly as Frank Tuttle wrote it. Because the author does not discuss every movie or television show he directed in the body of the text, I have included a complete chronological list of his film and television credits at the end of the book. In addition, all of the extant unpublished treatments, scenarios, screenplays, plays, and musical librettos written by Tuttle, alone and in collaboration with others, currently housed in the Tuttle Collection at the American Museum of the Moving Image in Astoria, New York, have been catalogued as well. Special thanks to Carey Stumm and Dana Nemeth for access to the materials. Many of the illustrations included in this volume were provided by Tuttle's daughter Helen Tuttle Votichenko whose generosity and enthusiasm facilitated the publication of her father's autobiography. Also included is an article Tuttle wrote entitled "Cleopatra and the Cobra," an expanded version of the Flore Revalles episode described in the autobiography.

Some years ago, film and television actor, Henry Gibson, related an experience he had in college: it seems that his work study assignment had been to drive the head of his department to and from the office and wherever else he needed to go. Gilbert V. Hartke, a former child actor in silent films, had become a Dominican priest, and even though the order required adherence to the vows of chastity, poverty, and obedience, Henry recalled that Hartke owned and drove a late model blue Cadillac. One day in the middle of the term, Henry summoned the courage to ask his boss how he could reconcile the vow of poverty with the possession of a new blue Cadillac. Without missing a beat, the former actor replied with great sincerity: "Blue. For the Blessed Mother."

Henry realized that he learned more about Father Hartke in that exchange than in an interpretative discussion of canonical vows. With the deftness of a magician—and spontaneity of a stand-up comedian—Hartke reminded Henry that he was not only a priest, but a performer as well.

With *They Started Talking*, Frank Tuttle performs a similar sleight of hand. By maintaining a tight focus on his career as a maker of movies, Tuttle offers us an amusement park ride through the film industry in the first half of the twentieth century when making movies was fun.

THEY STARTED TALKING
BY
FRANK TUTTLE

For

Teddy, Helen, and Barbara

and

Billie, who bullied me into writing this meandering monologue about moving pictures and me.

NOTE

The following account of my experiences as a moving picture director should explain itself but it might be wise to add that I shall say nothing about people and incidents which have not been associated with my work. There'll be no stories about my married life or my wonderful daughters and grandsons, and I'll mention only such happenings in my background and upbringing as have some bearing upon my career as a writer and director. In short, what follows will be an informal account of the movies as they affected the life of one director during some forty years of making them. There will be comments about his craft and his associates, plus whatever events seemed amusing or deserving a special word or two. And that will be it.

Frank Tuttle

CHAPTER 1

I hit the actor on the back of the head. "Harder!" he said. "That won't give me a headache." I slugged him again. "That's better," he said.

Hitting the actor was not the act of a sadist. Earlier, I had called my producer and told him I'd have to get his boy drunk and take other drastic measures to produce the effects of a hangover. Otherwise, his protégé just wasn't experienced enough to play the scene. The producer had given me his okay and sent me a bottle of scotch.

The next morning, the actor and I saw the rushes. They were pretty good. We returned to the set. The actor asked for a drink. I shook my head. "You don't need it," I said. "Today, you're an actor." He grinned and gave a better performance than the one he'd given with a real hangover.

Both of these tricks are what a movie director sometimes has to resort to.

I guess there's no way to avoid *The Children's Hour* in an autobiography, so here goes.

I was born in New York on August 6, 1892. One of my first memories is watching the parade celebrating Admiral Dewey's naval victory in the Spanish-American war. I was six.

My father, Fred Bradley Tuttle, was born in Lee, Massachusetts. He started as a civil engineer and ended as the president of the Tuttle Roofing Company, which also started and finished things. Father's company waterproofed the cellars and laid the roofs on the Empire State Building, the Hippodrome, and many other New York landmarks.

Before her marriage, my mother was Helen Hislop Dodds. Her father, Edmund Dodds, was a Scotsman who came to the United States during the administration of Franklin Pierce. Grandfather Dodds spoke with a bur-r-r until the day he died. Every morning, he greeted me and my sister Elizabeth with, "How's a' wi' ya?" to which we replied, "Brawley." Mother had planned to name me Edmund, but at the last moment father decided to call me Frank after his only brother. Grandfather Dodds retaliated by nicknaming me Donald MacDonald, and I was known as Donald until I was sent to the Hill School in Pottstown, Pennsylvania. In addition, grandfather won a post-mortem victory in the matter of my name. During World War II, I sent for my birth certificate, and there it was—Edmund Tuttle. Apparently the doctor had made it out and signed it before father decided to call me Frank.

Grandfather was a rabid Giant fan. He sat in the bleachers, and if the umpire made a decision he disagreed with, he rose, his white beard bristling, and shouted, "Take him oot!"

Mother's sister, Josephine Dodds, was a New York public school teacher and lived with us. She was a dear and remarkable woman, with a warm understanding and love for children. My sister Bess was older than I. Aunt Jo answered anything we asked her, an impressive accomplishment, but her knowledge seemed to be endless. She used to read the novels of Sir Walter Scott and James Fennimore Cooper to us, skillfully skipping over the dull passages. I was not quite ten when Aunt Jo began reading to us, which explains my early interest in literature.

Our family was divided into two camps. Mother, Aunt Jo, Bess, and I were all-out fans for books, the theatre, music, and dancing. Aunt Jo played the piano and mother sang. Father liked baseball, hunting, and fishing. He fell asleep at the theater. The jabber that accompanied our evening meals must have irked him no end. We talked endlessly about the lively arts. I was completely stage struck.

Incidentally, I am still amazed at my first creative attempt at the age of twelve. I wrote a parody of George M. Cohan's popular patriotic song, "You're a Grand Old Flag." What astounds me was its apparent sophistication. The only explanation I can think of for this, since I was actually completely naïve about the ways of the world, is that I had picked up a phony savoir-faire from attending the shows at the Colonial Theatre, then one of the outstanding theatres where vaudeville was king. Here's what I wrote:

> I've a grand old jag
> And I feel like a rag,
> And I look like an Indian brave.
> I'm the emblem of

> The drink I love—
> The cocktail about which I rave.
> Oh, the nightsticks beat true
> On my head a tattoo;
> The coppers won't let me lag.
> But should auld acquaintance be forgot?
> 'Taint the first time I've seen this jag!

How about that?

In her quiet way, my mother was an extraordinary woman, and I was an extraordinary daydreamer. Mother used to find my clothes in a disorderly pile on the floor. When she scolded me for my sloppiness, I stammered that I'd been thinking about something. It was years before she taught me to pick them up and put them where they belonged. Then, too, she had to prod me constantly to get me to school on time.

Mother was shy to the point of seeming to be afraid of people; but her shyness vanished when she stumbled upon cruelty. Then she became an avenging angel. If she saw a man beating a horse, she would rush up to him and let him have it with a blistering tirade. Any kind of violence upset her. Loud noises frightened her. During a thunderstorm she would hurry into the nearest closet and stay there until the storm was over. If Bess and I started a pillow fight, she would stop us and declare that "fooling always ends seriously!" She disliked any kind of rough competition. I was not allowed to have an air rifle until I was twelve. Another of her obsessions was that most mothers talked too much about their children and sang their praises excessively. Fearful that praise would inflate our egos, she seldom missed an opportunity to disparage our accomplishments. If I stumbled awkwardly or dropped something, she would exclaim that for a boy who did card tricks I was terribly clumsy. In my sophomore year, I was elected to Psi Upsilon. I called mother from New Haven to give her the glad tidings. After a moment's silence, she said, "I thought Psi U was a good fraternity."

Mother and Aunt Jo were very close. In most things their tastes were the same. They loved nature as much as they loved the theatre and music. Every summer, they collected samples of the flowers in Mrs. Dana's book, *How to Know the Wild Flowers*. Finally, they found every one she mentioned. Until I was twelve we spent our summers in New Marlboro, a tiny town in the Berkshires where mother and father had met. This was a beautiful spot with a village green, an old-fashioned country store, and not more than twenty houses. My companion was Louis Adsit, son of the country store's proprietor. We wandered about the countryside together. I particularly remember the local brook, the Glen, where we waded and scared the trout, then stretched out on the bank, our bodies dappled with leaf shadows. Those were fine days.

Frank Tuttle at home in Greenwich, Connecticut. From left, Frank's father, Fred, Aunt Jo, one of Frank's college friends, Frank's mother, Helen, Frank, his daughter Fredrika ("Teddy"), and his first wife, Fredericka.

Mother's and Aunt Jo's criticism of acting were very shrewd. If they caught an actor hamming it up, they gave one another "the Dodds look," as Bess and I christened a certain scathing facial expression, their reaction to anything phony or distasteful. They had both seen Edwin Booth perform, and they assured me that he was as modern as John Barrymore.

Between the ages of fifteen and sixteen, I shot up to over six feet. Bess taught me to dance and to play tennis. This was not an entirely altruistic move on her part, since it assured her of a partner if her charms failed elsewhere. And it was all right with me, until it dawned on me that what she had taught me made a hit with other members of the fair sex. Bess had a dry wit and loved to puncture my foibles. Like most hams, I behaved with a certain show-off style which frequently covered up a lack of real ability. Bess described this trait with scathing truthfulness. "Frank," she said. "You have the gestures for everything!"

Father and I had little in common except fishing. After my graduation, we made several springtime safaris to Hartsville, a village close to New Marlboro, where a friend of father's since his boyhood was Bert Whitney, the blacksmith. We drove there from Greenwich in my Model T Ford. We got up at five-thirty every morning, prepared three package lunches, and fished until late afternoon. Father always bagged the most trout. With infinite care and patience, he would crawl to the bank of the brook and let the current carry the baited hook to the ripples at the edge of what looked like a promising hole. If a trout struck, father would give it some slack, set the hook in the fish's mouth with a quick jerk, then reel it in until the trout was close enough to the shore so that he could land it and pounce upon it. I watched him accomplish the trick many times, but I never mastered it. More often than not, my hook and line would get tangled in the leaves of a tree branch or a bush; but I enjoyed the sport, and when I became disgusted with my frequent failures I would stretch out on the good New England earth and daydream, just as I had when I was a youngster.

For all our temperamental differences, father was very fond of me and put up with my love for things theatrical with remarkable tolerance. He was a living example of the strong, silent man. One day, before I had learned how to swim, he was carrying me on his shoulder, knee-deep in the surf at Coney Island. An unexpected giant wave knocked him down. When he fished me out of the undertow, I was much too astonished that anything could have belted father off his feet to cry. This pleased him.

On my own, I was terrified of getting hurt. In the early days of my childhood we lived close to some tough neighborhoods and I never had a fight. I was too scared. I was over thirty when I took my first boxing lesson, which I forced myself to do as an antidote to cowardice. I was forty-five when I first rode a horse. Then I did it the hard way. I hired a Hollywood Cossack stunt rider to teach me. In two lessons he had me galloping and eventually taught me to jump.

Though my mother and my aunt were deeply concerned with the American Negro's struggle to improve his lot, father had very little sympathy for Negroes or other minorities. With his family, he was gentle and considerate, but in the business world he was inclined to be intolerant and ruthless. He had no use for labor unions. They cut into his profits.

When he was eighty-six, shortly before he died, he came to Hollywood and spent several days on the set of the picture I was directing. He was impressed with the respect the actors, assistants, and technicians showed for me, and, I think, considerably surprised. One evening, I arranged for a small poker party at my house. Among the players were Bill Powell, a good friend of mine, and Sol Siegel, at that time the Paramount producer of the picture I was directing. I had a great respect and liking for my boss. Father was an excellent poker player—and lucky. He won. He suddenly decided that movie people, whom he had always regarded as a kind of necessary evil to entertain women and children, were great guys.

As you can see from what I've written about, for the most part my childhood was an extremely happy one, due largely to three wonderful women: my mother, my aunt, and my sister.

CHAPTER 2

In a roundabout way, my breaking into moving pictures began in New York at the Coffee House, a men's luncheon club founded in 1916 by Frank Crowninshield and a group of writers, architects, editors, actors, and others connected with the arts.

Following my graduation from Yale in 1915, my first job was as Crowninshield's assistant editor. He had been chosen as the editor of *Vanity Fair* a few years before by publisher Condé Nast. Crowninshield had quickly stamped the magazine with his sophisticated exploitation of the foibles of the New York of that period. His contributors included Robert Benchley, P.G. Wodehouse, Stephen Leacock, and Dorothy Parker, whom I remember as a wide-eyed youngster who had just deposited some samples of her verse on Crowny's desk. One of them spoke of the female impersonator, Julian Eltinge, and rhymed "ambidextrous" with "ambisextrous." Crowninshield signed her on the spot. I believe it is fair to say that Crowny's *Vanity Fair* was a forerunner of *The New Yorker*. He modestly described the magazine as a picture book in the sense that the British fortnightlies, *The Sketch* and *The Tatler*, were picture books with photographs of current personalities of society, the theatre, sports, and the cinema.

My contribution was caption writing, describing the pictured personalities with a humorous touch and writing quips to go under sketches by Ethel Plummer, Clara Tice, and others. My salary was thirty dollars a week.

After about a year of this, Frank Crowninshield fired me. Publisher Nast felt that he needed a different kind of assistant, an experienced editor who could take the mechanics of editing off Frank's shoulders and leave him free to find new, young talent—to move about in New York's Café

Frank and friends at *Vanity Fair*.

Society, where Frank knew everyone. When he gave me the sack, Crowny was sincerely distressed. He wrote stacks of amusing letters urging his friends to hire me.

I tried my hand at being a press agent, that "pirate on the high seas of journalism," as Walter Kingsley, publicity chief for the Palace Theatre, dubbed the members of his profession. My first offer came from Edward L. Bernays, who is today one of the most eminent experts in the field of public relations. When I asked him for a job, he was promoting the Diaghilev Ballets Russes, which was soon to make its first appearance in the United States with the "Great Nijinsky." Eddie Bernays asked me if I could type. When I told him I couldn't he shook his head and explained that this was an absolute necessity. I went home and for one grueling week I sat at a typewriter and learned the touch system. The following Monday I got the job.

When the ballet troupe arrived, I watched several rehearsals and became a balletomane in nothing flat. My coup d'état as a press agent involved Mlle. Flore Revalles, a Swiss opera singer whom Léon Bakst had persuaded Diaghilev to engage because he visualized her in the costumes he had designed for *Cléopâtre* and Zobeide in *Scheherazade*. As neither of these roles was performed on toe, Diaghilev said yes.

Eddie Bernays gave me carte blanche to try the publicity stunt if I could persuade Mlle. Revalles to cooperate. First, I hustled to the Bronx Zoo to sell the idea to Mr. Snyder, the curator of the reptile house. I explained to him that if I could talk our Swiss Miss into being photographed with a live snake, we could say that she was studying the movements of a cobra for her dance. Snyder pointed out that we could use a non-poisonous king snake because the cobra only spreads its hood when it is angry, and the American king snake would make a perfect double in all other respects.

Back in the city I made my pitch to the lovely Flore in my brokendown Yale French, and she agreed to get a friend to motor her to the zoo the following Sunday. I had chosen Sunday because there are less visitors on paydays. When our entourage arrived, Mr. Snyder donated his office as a dressing room. While our star was changing, I explained to the curator and the still cameraman that if all else failed it might be necessary for Snyder to hold the snake. He grinned and agreed. When Cleopatra appeared in the diaphanous Bakst outfit we walked to the glass enclosure where several king snakes dripped, intertwined, from leafless tree branches.

Snyder asked the Queen of the Nile which reptile she would prefer. She indicated the largest one. Snyder nodded and entered the enclosure. I remember expecting him to do something or other with a forked stick, but he simply reached over and entwined the six-foot snake, which continually flicked out its tongue. When he joined us with his prize he explained that the reptile would never stop moving, but that all Mlle. Revalles had to do was reach out and grasp it with her free hand. Before he finished his little lecture, Cleopatra had the snake. It slithered slowly up on her arm and across her naked back. "Ah-h," she said, her eyes gleaming, "*C'est délicieux!*"

We went outdoors and took our pictures. In one of them, the still man snapped his graflex just before the snake reached her face, which she turned aside as the reptile glided once more across her shoulders.

Recently, I had dinner with the Bernays family in New York and Eddie showed me a huge scrapbook which was completely filled with newspaper clippings of Flore Revalles and her pet "cobra."

When the ballet company started its coast-to-coast tour, I accompanied the troupe as far as New Haven. Here, I was privileged to escort Nijinsky and his wife, Romula, around the campus of Yale University. When we paused before the statue of Nathan Hale which stands in front of Connecticut Hall, I explained that Hale had roomed here as a student before the American Revolution. I went on to tell how he had been captured by the British during the war and hanged as a spy. I ended the harangue by quoting Hale's immortal, "My only regret is that I have but one life to give for my country." Nijinsky digested my recital for some time then remarked in French, "Hmm. Did he give it?"

Shortly after this my job with the Ballets Russes ended. With the help of Eddie Bernays, I got a position as the publicity representative for the New York Philharmonic Orchestra. The manager of the Philharmonic, Felix Leifels, proved to be as kind and wonderful a friend as Frank Crowninshield had been. At the end of a year I had my work simplified to a point where I could write the press releases and certain letters which Leifels felt needed polishing during the mornings, and spend my afternoons writing short stories and plays, which Leifels encouraged me to plug away at.

Meanwhile, Crowny had arranged to have me elected to the Coffee House Club. This brings me back to my introduction to the world of motion pictures. In my brief dedication I mentioned that this would be a meandering monologue, but from now on I believe I'll be able to stick more closely to the chronology of things as they happened.

Anxious to rub elbows with the Coffee House greats, I lunched quite frequently at the Club. Another new member there was Walter Wanger. Shortly after his graduation from Dartmouth, he had produced several plays with Alla Nazimova as the star. Now, still in his twenties, he had become the East Coast production head of Paramount Pictures.

One day at the Club I suggested to Wanger that I'd like to try my hand at adapting material owned by Paramount into treatment form and asked him to let me have some plays and novels to work on during my free afternoons. Walter thought this an excellent idea and said he'd discuss it with his colleagues and let me know how they felt about it the next time we had lunch together.

Later that week, we met again and Wanger reported a new development. Charles Maigne, one of Paramount's West Coast directors, had arrived in New York to direct Thomas Meighan in *The Frontier of the Stars*. Maigne was looking for a young writer whom he could train to prepare scripts for him. He had been a writer before he started to direct. Walter had set up a meeting between Maigne and me for that afternoon at the Lambs Club. I was to take along some samples of my writing. I stammered my thanks and dashed back to Carnegie Hall where Felix Leifels and I made a frantic selection of plays, short stories, and articles I'd written for *Vanity Fair*. I grabbed a cab and took off for the Lambs.

Maigne was an able and experienced director. He had once been an army man and gave the impression of being pretty cynical and hardboiled. We had a drink and he spoke enthusiastically about James Branch Cabell's novel, *Jurger*, and I agreed that Cabell was a fine writer as I shoveled my brain-children out of the briefcase. He started to read. I gulped my Scotch. By the time we'd had four I was dishing out the best of Crowny's bon mots and Maigne was grinning. One drink later he declared that I was exactly what he was looking for.

The next day, Wanger called me and confirmed this. After a month's tryout with Maigne while he was shooting *The Frontier of the Stars* at the old Biograph studio, I was to get a year's contract at a hundred dollars a week if I had proved satisfactory during the tryout.

For the first two weeks, I watched Maigne direct Thomas Meighan and his leading lady, Faire Binney, lunched with the director and the cast, and read all the screenplays I could lay my hands on. Then I got jumpy.

Obviously Maigne would have no more idea about my screen writing ability when option time came due than he had when he had told Wanger to try me out. As Mr. Samuel Goldwyn said to Eddie Cantor many years later when I was directing *Roman Scandals*, I decided to "take the bull between my teeth." I announced that I had started writing the screenplay of Maigne's next picture, *The Kentuckians*, which would be adapted from the novel by John Fox, Jr. Maigne said that was fine.

With the help of the director's secretary, Ethel Brush, I went to work. She coached me thoroughly in the technique of screenplay writing. Soon I was glibly dictating words like subtitle, spoken title, fade in, fade out, and dissolve.

When the month was up, Wanger checked with Maigne. The director told him I was great. On his say-so, Paramount took up my option. Actually, Maigne had not read one word I had written. A month or so later he did read my script. He made no comment but started casting before taking off for Big Stone Gap, Virginia, the first location for *The Kentuckians*. Apparently he thought my screenplay was a workable vehicle and was actually going to shoot it. Believe it or not, he did.

In Virginia, however, after a few days' work with Monte Blue, who was playing Boone Stallard, John Fox, Jr.'s hero, Maigne discovered a hole in the script's structure. Working nights, he dictated his revisions to Miss Brush. I read them and agreed that they were a vast improvement. The shooting continued. The camera equipment in those days had reached a pretty high standard. Until the advent of the talkies, most of the improvements made before that radical change were in the lenses and the sensitivity of the film itself. Maigne finished with the Big Stone Gap location in less than two weeks. The company moved onto Lexington, Kentucky. I was sent back to New York. Charles Maigne took no credit for his screenplay doctoring.

At this point an explanation seems due. Otherwise someone might jump to the conclusion that this neophyte, whose first screenplay was actually photographed by an established director with only one major job of rewriting, must have been touched with genius. Far from it. The real explanation of the apparent miracle lies in the fact that I was not quite as inexperienced as what I have written seems to indicate. There is a gap in my account which I should have filled in. So I'll have to meander again. I'll have to fall back on something that was in practically every screenplay in those days—a flashback.

CHAPTER 3

At college I had majored in English and concentrated on playwriting. Professor Baker's course was still at Harvard, but Yale had a fine drama teacher, Jack Crawford. Our textbook was the William Archer classic on the subject. Jack's students experimented with play outlines, and we wrote several one set plays.

I was also active with the Yale University Dramatic Association as an actor. Monty Woolley coached the plays we toured in during the Christmas holidays and the spring play which was performed in an outdoor theatre during commencement. One of my classmates was Charles Andrew Merz, until recently editorial page editor of *The New York Times*, a position he held for twenty-five years.

During one summer vacation we collaborated on a dramatization of Sir Walter Scott's *Quentin Durward*. Due largely to the enthusiasm of Professor William Lyon Phelps, the "Dramat" accepted our play and it was presented as the Association's spring production in 1914. Monty Woolley was far from sharing Professor Phelps' enthusiasm-and with reason. *Quentin Durward*, with its "How nows?" and its "What means this blare of martial trumpets?" was definitely way down yonder in the cornfield. During the preceding Christmas week "Dramat" tour, one of the plays presented had been *Gringoire*, which told the story of a starving French poet pleading for the poverty-stricken people of Paris with King Louis XI of France. Louis had been excellently played by Stoddard King, who won national fame in 1917 when he wrote the lyrics of "There's a Long, Long Trail a Winding." Since King Louis would be an important character in *Quentin Durward*, Monty suggested to Doc Merz and me that we give Stoddard King a stirring speech similar to the one he had delivered in *Gringoire*. We took his advice. The captain of the Yale fencing team was also persuaded to stage some exciting swordplay for Quentin and the villain of our piece, William de la Mark, "the Wild Boar of the Ardennes." We also added a musical introduction by another classmate, Douglas Stuart Moore, who is today the head of the music department at Columbia University, and one of America's top-ranking composers. In his sophomore year, Doug had written the words and music for "Good Night Poor Harvard."

From the program notes, the commencement audience could discover that this was the first Dramatic Association production written by undergraduates, which, I have always suspected, led them to give our solo performance of *Quentin Durward* a warmer reception than it deserved. To put it bluntly, no one asked for his money back.

In my senior year, I was the President of the "Dramat." We presented a series of one-acters for our Christmas week tour. I tried my hand again as a playwright with a melodrama, *Saint Bartholomew's Eve*. I shudder when I think of it. Monty Woolley shuddered too, but luckily for me, he was too smart to be caught by another "tuttlety." He rushed for help to Professor John Berdan, a fine teacher and an excellent writer. With infinite tact, Berdan gradually made me realize that my one-acter was badly in need of a rewrite. He went to work and came up with a charming substitute in which nothing remained of the original except the title. Happily, for the "Dramat," another undergraduate, Almet Jenks, had written a fine short tragedy, *The Stranger*. When our season opened, Almet's pay scored an immediate hit and Professor Berdan's version of *Saint Bartholomew's Eve* was well received too. Berdan insisted on taking no credit for his play. The situation was saved and I had shamefacedly learned that it takes more than youthful enthusiasm to create for the theatre.

My next adventure with playwriting came just after I started my job as the publicity representative for the New York Philharmonic.

For many years, the outstanding amateur acting organization in New York was the Comedy Club. Several of its members eventually became professionals. Among its talented performers were Harold Gould, Theodore Steinway, Henry Clapp Smith, Sterling Foote, and Austin Strong, the playwright. Austin staged several shows for the club as a prelude to directing his own plays. In 1917 his *Three Wise Fools* was running on Broadway and a year later, he wrote the smash hit, *Seventh Heaven*. Just before I left *Vanity Fair*, I joined the Comedy Club as an amateur actor.

Frank and daughter Fredrika ("Teddy") in Greenwich, Connecticut, 1918.

Shortly after this, I finished the first draft of a satiric comedy about the phony artists in Greenwich Village. I submitted the play to the Comedy Club. Its play committee thought it contained some amusing scenes and finally agreed to do it if Austin Strong would direct it. Austin was also a member of the Coffee House Club. After lunch one day he told me he had read the play and would direct it on one condition. I would have to accept him as the absolute final authority and make any revisions he suggested without question. I agreed. Austin told me that my work showed promise but he felt that I needed the rough handling writers frequently get in the professional theatre. I said I'd be delighted to be put through the mill.

When rehearsals started they took place at night because the club members all had daytime jobs. After several readings, Austin took me aside, slapped his script in front of me and pointed to a scene. "This should come earlier," he said. "Here!" I was flabbergasted. "But, Austin—" I said. He cut me short with, "Bring me the rewrite Monday." I swallowed and nodded. Over the weekend I discovered he was right and found a way to do what he wanted. He accepted the revision without comment. At a later rehearsal he indicated a long speech by my artist hero. "Cut the hell out of that," he said. "He talks like a drunken Baptist." I made the changes during the rehearsal. Austin grinned at my drastic blue-penciling. "You're listening," he said. His dynamic personality inspired the actors and made them believe that the material was superlatively good. He never criticized the writing except when he and I were alone. Then he would toss off a variety of exciting ideas.

Austin believed that the eye reacted much more quickly and critically to what was happening on the stage than the ear. "Instead of talking about honesty," he said, "it's usually much more effective to point to a picture of Lincoln." This kind of thinking was particularly helpful to someone who was going to start his career as a writer for moving pictures. Austin had a good many theories about the technique of playwriting. He was convinced, for instance, that a play wasn't really a play unless it contained a "cause of action." He illustrated what this was with a syllogism, using *Romeo and Juliet* as an example. He stated the basic structure of *Romeo* as follows. Condition of action: a boy and girl of feuding families in love. Cause of action: they marry. "Notice," Austin said, "that until this happens the situation might go on indefinitely." The cause of action meshes the gears and starts things moving. Result of action. This is always stated as a question, thus: will the marriage result in bringing the two families together? Will it produce a tragedy? Or will it do both?

Austin would talk about his theories eloquently, while I listened like one of the boys in the back room with Socrates.

If Austin had a weakness, I believe it was his indifference to what William Archer called the "drama of ideas." Austin Strong's plays were exciting, moving, and effective, but they were seldom touched with profundity. I should point out once again that this was not too important for a pupil who was going to write silent picture screenplays. Until pictures started talking, serious comments on life were extremely rare. What Shaw called "the discussion" was practically non-existent in the days of the "silents." Pictures like *Intolerance* did carry a message but it was pretty well buried in the melodrama and the spectacle.

Finally, *The Village*, started its limited run at the old Madison Square Garden Theatre. The audience reaction was extremely gratifying. To hear people laugh at something you've given a character to say is balm to the author's ego, to say the least. One member of the Comedy Club had an "in" with the press and some of New York's second-string critics came to see the show. They were kind. One of them compared my comedy with Sinclair Lewis' *Hobohemia* and the comparison was not at all odious, particularly since the Lewis play was running professionally on Broadway. His words of praise bucked me up tremendously.

A few days after we closed, Austin handed me a few typewritten pages entitled "Some Words of Advice from an Old Hack to a Budding Genius." It was an analysis of my approach to playwriting. He let me have it with both barrels. I winced as I read it, but eventually Austin's words of wisdom had a most salutary effect. I imagine they were largely responsible for my doing as well as I did with *The Kentuckians*. Later in my professional career I asked for Austin's help when something in a script bothered me and I was stuck. He always came through with a heartwarming assist. A real friend in need.

End of flashback.

When I returned to New York from Big Stone Gap, I reported to Tom Geraghty, the head of the scenario department at Paramount's Long Island studio.

Geraghty had started his writing career as a newspaperman and was well known in Hollywood as a fine scenarist, particularly because of several outstanding screenplays he had written for Douglas Fairbanks, Sr.

Frank and his wife, Fredericka, on a camping trip with director George Stevens and his wife.

His forte was comedy-drama, but he was an excellent judge of picture writing in all its phases. He gave shrewd advice and criticism to the Eastern staff of writers at Paramount's Astoria studio, and they loved working for him. I can still see him puffing on a cigar stub and muttering, "Look. You can cut out all that big build-up of Richard Dix as an honest man. He's been honest for years. Now if you started him as a crook—." Unlike Austin Strong, Tom never theorized about story structure or anything else. He seemed to snatch ideas from nowhere and apply them instinctively; and they were consistently fresh and effective.

The morning after I got back from *The Kentuckians'* location, Geraghty had asked all the writers to drop into his office. He distributed copies of a screenplay written on the West Coast for Thomas Meighan. It was based on Booth Tarkington's *The Conquest of Canaan*. The picture would be shot in the East. Geraghty was not too happy with the script and asked us all to report any suggestions we might have for a rewrite as soon as we'd read it.

Everyone but me was an established screenwriter and already involved in a project. On my way home I suddenly realized that this could be an opening. I read the script that night. The following morning I was in Geraghty's office at 9:15 with a flock of ideas. Puffing on the cigar stub, he listened attentively, made a few amusing suggestions, and gave me the job.

The assignment turned out to be a real break in more ways than one. When Charles Maigne got back from Lexington, he finished shooting the interiors of *The Kentuckians* and editing it. Then he got into a hassle with the front office about the next picture they had scheduled him to direct. The upshot of the disagreement was that he quit. Because I was working on the Tarkington script I stayed on. If I'd been Maigne's new boy, without an assignment, I would undoubtedly have been fired. Sheer luck.

Luck is a strange intangible. Most of us are inclined to believe that our success is largely due to our ability. Only bad luck, we assume, is fate. My experience has led me to believe the opposite. Of course the breaks do work both ways. Certainly in the case of my having a job when Maigne quit, they worked for me; but for the most part, a detached appraisal seems to indicate that we should blame ourselves when we stub our toes and give the credit to Lady Luck when that golden opportunity comes from left field. Mixed metaphors, anyone?

After finishing and revising the screenplay of *The Conquest of Canaan* under Tom Geraghty's watchful guidance, I was sent with the company to Asheville, North Carolina. Paramount's location department had chosen Asheville because it was early spring and we needed a small town and good weather. To find such a place within striking distance of New York was a problem. In California, the big studios have a variety of exterior sets standing on their back lots, and practically every imaginable outdoor setting is close at hand. I need hardly add that for three quarters of the year good weather is guaranteed by the Chamber of Commerce.

Thomas Meighan's leading lady was Doris Kenyon and the director was Roy Neill. Neill was short, dynamic—in his middle thirties. He was not one of the greats of the period but he knew his business thoroughly and I learned a lot watching him work. For example, he was one of the first directors to use an innovation introduced by Erich von Stroheim, the movement of passersby between the actors and the camera, thus heightening the illusion that the scene was really happening. In the movies of this period the sense of reality had already been contributed to by the movability of the camera and D.W. Griffith's discovery of the close-up. In the theatre, actors have to project vocally and facially to be effective beyond the first few rows. It soon became apparent to picture makers that honest thinking photographed. Contrary to the common belief, actors found they could project thoughts and emotions with less "mugging" for the camera than was necessary to put over a point for a live audience.

Thomas Meighan was an experienced and successful stage actor, but he was even more effective in front of a camera. He meant what he was doing and this sincerity came over perfectly. His life was normal. He was happily married. He was talented. All this photographed. When he wasn't working his quiet, Irish humor was a delight. I remember standing with him in front of a huge fireplace in the Asheville Hotel. He pointed to the gigantic area and remarked without smiling, "What a spot for a 'vision,' hmm?"

In those days there were no talent guilds and "on-location" the director's assistant lured the all too willing spectators into walking through the scenes. Roy Neill made spectacular capital of this. One sequence in the script called for the crowd to storm the courthouse. Neill shot all the medium and close set-ups first, his camera angled toward the building. During these preliminaries, Roy's assistants and the local police roped off the spectators who had come for miles to watch us. Meanwhile Roy had a second camera ready to set up inside the doorway, shooting toward the watching crowd. Incidentally, the camera of that period was hand-cranked. The motor-driven camera was introduced several years later. As soon as the second cameraman was ready and signaled the assistants, they dropped the ropes and urged the watchers forward. Led by the actors who were not in this sequence and the shouting assistants, the milling hundreds stormed the courthouse as though it were the Bastille. Back at Astoria, several weeks later, we saw the scene in the Paramount projection room. It was a dilly.

CHAPTER 4

When we returned from Asheville, I was delighted to discover that Monty Woolley was being groomed to be a Paramount director. He got the chance through Bill Bullitt, another Yale graduate who was now a front office executive. He was the William Christian Bullitt who later became our first ambassador to Russia after the Soviet Union had been recognized by our Government.

Monty started out doing minor directorial chores. Among them was *Bullets or Ballots*, an educational short. The actors were asked to contribute their services. This made Monty's job a particularly tough one, since most of them were either young hopefuls or just a degree more talented than extras. Since I was between assignments, I volunteered to work as Monty's assistant. The heroine of the one-reeler was played by Mary Astor, who was fifteen, talented, and a real beauty. Monty had to use sets that were already standing and take whatever he could beg, borrow, or steal in the way of technical help. Despite these obstacles, he did a fine job.

When the shooting was finished, I attached myself to the cutter, eager to find out what I could about this important phase of picture making. I soon discovered that the great trick in putting together long shots, medium shots, and close-ups, is to make the transition from one angle to another as smooth as possible, so that the viewer is hardly conscious of the change. The cutter was a helpful and humorous pal. He even went so far as to let me try my hand at assembling and splicing a segment of the film. It's a real kick to go into a projection room and watch the brief running of what you've patched together. My instructor generously taught me the basic essentials of his job. As you can imagine, this was a tremendous asset to me later.

Shortly after this and before I'd been given a writing assignment, Paramount's Eastern studio closed down for several months and I was out of a job. I told myself that at least I was now an established screenwriter, but I was pretty scared.

[Here a page from Tuttle's manuscript is missing. Newspaper reports indicate that the closing of Paramount's Eastern studio was strangely fortuitous for Tuttle since it prompted him to create his own production company, Patuwa Pictures, capitalized at $20,000 and incorporated on October 4, 1921 in partnership with Fred Waller, Jr., an illustrator and photographer. Almost immediately, the new company began producing films as the "Film Guild." Modeled after the Theatre Guild, and formed to provide an alternative to epic-scale movie spectaculars with highly detailed, realistic settings, the Film Guild was a profit-sharing, cooperative organization idealistically designed to make "swift, impressionistic pictures" that "place sincere, fundamentally true stories and acting above everything else." On November 27, 1921, the *New York Times* announced that the company's first film, *Apron Strings*, written and directed by Frank Tuttle, was in production with Glenn Hunter as the leading man, and the following March, the *Times* advertised the official incorporation of the company capitalized at $50,000 and listed Tuttle, Waller, and Dwight Wiman (a former vice-president of the Yale Dramatic Club) as the founding partners. On May 28, the day prior to the premiere of *Apron Strings* (retitled *The Cradle Buster*) at the Cameo in New York City, the *Times* added Townsend Martin (a former president of the Princeton Dramatic Club), Osgood Perkins (a member of the Harvard Hasty Pudding Club), and James A. Creelman (a film scenarist and former editor of *The Yale Record*) to the team. Where the narrative in the manuscript continues, Tuttle relates the hazards in raising the capital necessary to produce the film.]

The next few weeks were bedlam. Glenn Hunter read my yarn and agreed to play the part and work for a minimum salary; but raising the $25,000 we needed to shoot the picture was something else again. It was really rugged. I approached a young friend of mine, Townsend Martin. He was a member of the Coffee House Club and quite well-to-do. He turned me down as an investor, but he'd done some acting and writing at Princeton and said he'd be interested in a chance to learn something about those departments of the movie business. I found a secondary role he could play, secretly hoping that once he'd got his feet wet he might still invest. Another friend I'd met the previous summer had been the star of Harvard's Hasty Pudding Club shows. Shortly after we met, we had appeared together in a charity show. He was a terrific actor. This young man was sharp featured, almost sinister-looking, and used his hands with striking expressiveness. The heavy in my story was the clown in an amusement part, "Cracked" Spooney. With our limited funds it would be impossible to get an experienced pro to play this important role. I asked my Harvard friend to play the part. Osgood Perkins agreed. Today few people know that the star of *The Front Page* and innumerable other Broadway shows (and the father of Tony Perkins) got his start as a moving picture actor.

In October we were confronted with a real dilemma. Our script called for a roller coaster sequence which would be shot in an amusement park. Of the $25,000 we had to have to make the picture, we raised $500. The leaves were beginning to fall. Fred Waller and I held a frantic conference. We decided to spend what we had to shoot the exteriors in the park, cut the sequence, and gamble on getting the rest of the money with this short episode to show to possible investors. We did this and shut up shop.

My father, who had already worked my way through college, came through with a very considerable hunk of dough. When I think about this in retrospect, I realize what this must have meant to him. He had no sympathy for my project and as a businessman, he certainly had no idea that his "investment" would eventually result in my becoming a well-paid director; but I was his son and had asked for his help. For my father that was enough. On the strength of his contribution I raised the rest from a group of my classmates. Eventually they got their money back but it wasn't until I went back to work at Paramount that I was able to reimburse them from my salary.

We shot the picture in about four weeks. During the shooting, we found out that a recognized writer had a story in a national magazine called *Apron Strings*. Charles Maigne's secretary, Ethel Brush, had lost her job when he left Paramount and we had given her the job of script clerk. This consists in noting the action in every take in detail so that the director and the cutter have a record of such tiny items as which hand was holding the cigarette when the actor exited from a scene so that it will match when he makes his entrance in the next cut, which may be photographed weeks later. She must also check his costume and the tempo with which the actor leaves the scene. Good script clerks are a great asset, and they take a vital interest in everything that goes on. When Ethel heard that we couldn't use *Apron Strings* as our title, she suggested that we call our picture *The Cradle Buster*, and that was its title when it was released.

Since this was my first time at bat as a director, the shooting and the camera angles were quite routine and deserve no comment except for one incident. The heroine of our story was the amusement park's tightrope walker, played by Marguerite Courtot, an excellent young actress who had just finished the lead in *Down to the Sea in Ships*. A professional high-wire walker doubled for Miss Courtot in the long shots. I dreamed up a gimmick to make it look as though our leading lady were actually on the tightrope. When I told my idea to Fred Waller he thought it was great. I need hardly add that I thought so too.

The background behind the tightrope was black. In front of this the grips rigged a springboard covered with black velvet. Parallel to the springboard, on the side facing the camera, they stretched a white rope and attached a nail to the board just above the rope. Miss Courtot, imitating the high-wire double's style, moved along on the black springboard. Her weight caused the white rope, pushed by the nail, to go up and down exactly as though she were on it, and we were so close that there could be no doubt that the wire walker was Marguerite Courtot. I had met the mother of the invention.

When the picture was finished, the toughest problem was still ahead of us—the distribution and release. The cutting had not been too difficult. With our scanty funds there was very little extra footage and, thanks to what I had learned from Paramount's cutter, I got the job done in jig time.

Just as I was splicing the last few frames, luck showed up once more in the person of Dwight Deere Wiman, of the John Deere Plow Company family. Dwight's older brother, Charles Deere Wiman, had been one of my roommates at college and was being groomed to become the future head of the company. This left Dwight free to come to New York and look for an entrée to Broadway. Like me, he had acted in a number of "Dramat" plays and like me, he was stage-struck. We ran *The Cradle Buster* for Dwight and he liked it. In fact, he offered to put up the money for a week's showing at the Cameo Theatre, so that we'd have some press notices and, if they were good, we could use them to help us get a distribution contract. Thanks to Dwight and some excellent reviews which praised the picture, we got our release. This was lucky for all of us and the experience of the next few years eventually led to Dwight's becoming a top Broadway producer.

Once the distribution deal was set, our next step was to form a producing company, which we called the Film Guild. In addition to me, its members included Glenn Hunter, Fred Waller, Osgood Perkins, Townsend Martin, and James Ashmore Creelman. Jim was a Yale graduate and the personal press representative for John Emerson and Anita Loos. He had also worked on several screenplays with them. We cooked up a series of pictures starring Glenn. Among them were *Second Fiddle, Youthful Cheaters, Grit,* and Percy MacKaye's, *The Scarecrow*. Dwight and Fred were in charge of the business end of the company, Glenn its star, and Osgood its character man. I directed the pictures and worked with Townsend and Jim on the writing. Jim was also in charge of Film Guild publicity. He wrote and planted a number of excellent press releases for us.

Mary Astor was Glenn's leading lady in *Second Fiddle* and *The Scarecrow*. At sixteen this lovely youngster was a tomboy but she was a fine trouper and extremely bright. During the shooting of silent movies, a three-piece orchestra played between takes as a morale booster and during dramatic scenes to help the actors emote. One day Mary suggested that they play a gay tune while she was doing a sad scene. She thought that acting against the mood of the music might be a challenge. I'm sure she would have given a good performance even with the conventional mood music. In any case, for Mary it worked perfectly. Aside from her good looks and her talent, Mary was the kind of person who never stopped asking questions about every phase of picture making. She was extremely self-critical and blessed with an abounding vitality.

Grit was written for the screen by Jim Creelman from an original story idea by F. Scott Fitzgerald, who was a classmate of Townsend Martin. In this picture, Glenn's leading lady was the fifteen-year-old Clara Bow. Anyone who ever worked with her will tell you that she was one of the most arresting personalities the screen has ever known. Born in the Brooklyn slums, this dynamic and erratic whirlwind was a joy to her director. You—and Clara—were never quite sure what was going to happen. One day, during the shooting of *Grit* she'd been clowning around just before a take. I ran through the scene with her. She parked her chewing gum and said, "Want me to cry?" I nodded. "Let's shoot it," she said. Seconds later, the tears were streaming down her cheeks. Stanislavski my eye!

Tuttle's daughters Fredrika ("Teddy") and Helen in Greenwich, Connecticut, 1924.

Like everyone who was privileged to direct Clara, I remember dozens of anecdotes, but there's one I must tell you right now although it occurred many years after *Grit*.

When pictures started talking, Clara was terrified. Actually she read her lines—she called them titles—with a sure instinct for what was right for Clara Bow; but she drove the sound crew crazy because her voice in the take wasn't even remotely like the rehearsal. The picture in which this anecdote happened was *No Limit*. I arrived at the studio one morning without a worry in the world because our first scene was one in which Clara was being married to Norman Foster. All she had to do was repeat the responses after the Reverend Neil Dodd, a real minister, who gave his check to the church.

My assistant grabbed me as I walked on the set and whispered ominously, "Miss Bow wants to see you, Frank!" I dashed into Clara's dressing room. She looked particularly lovely in the wedding gown Edith Head had designed for her, but she was one jump this side of hysterics. She told me that she couldn't make a word of sense out of what she was supposed to say, and that the extras thought she was a dumb jerk. I said she was nuts. They thought she was terrific and she was. She stifled a sob and shoved her script at me. "What does that mean?" she said. I took a quick look at, "I, Rose, take thee, David, to my lawful wedded husband." I came up with a forced grin. "That's just an old-fashioned way of saying, 'take you to *be* my wedded husband,'" I said. No soap. She tried it and stuttered like Roscoe Ates. Her panic had completely inhibited her. Suddenly inspired by the thought of what the delay was costing us, I told her we'd shoot the part of the service where Norman Foster read the responses. I could feel the terror oozing out of her pores. "That's it," I said. "See you on the set in ten minutes!" And I made a flying exit.

I held a hurried conference with Norman and the Reverend Dodd. I was figuring out something.

At the end of the first take Clara's eyes were misty. "Let's do it just once more," I said and squeezed Dodd's arm. In the next take when Norman finished, Clara's eyes were brimming. She looked at her husband-to-be with love everlasting. The minister turned to her. "Now, Rose," he said, "Repeat after me, 'I, Rose, take thee, David—.'" I held my breath. Then a tremulous voice whispered. "I, Rose, take thee, David, to my lawful wedded husband—." A pause. Then a shriek. "Jeez!" exclaimed Clara, "I said it!"

CHAPTER 5

The good ship Film Guild finally foundered when Glenn Hunter left us. His appearance in the Kaufman-Connelly play, *Merton of the Movies*, won him Broadway stardom and later he appeared in the movie version. The rest of us made a few historical pictures for a series produced by Yale University. After this we folded our tents like the Arabs. Dwight Wiman and Osgood Perkins stole away to the theatre, Jim Creelman returned to the Emerson-Loos Company, and Fred Waller and I went back to Paramount, which had reopened. My return was arranged through Lloyd Sheldon, the new head of Paramount's Eastern story department. He had sold a number of original screenplays and stories to Paramount and was their logical choice to succeed Tom Geraghty, who had gone back to Hollywood. The assignment Sheldon had for me was a chore any writer would have been delighted to get.

Director Allan Dwan was the man actually responsible for my landing the job. It seems he had heard about my sudden switch from writing to directing when Paramount closed down. Apparently he was impressed by my brashness. In any case, he had asked Lloyd to see if I were available as the writer for his next picture, *Manhandled*.

Dwan was a top-flight director and he still is. At that time his best-known picture was the Douglas Fairbanks spectacular, *Robin Hood*. When I told him how much I had been impressed by his direction of that wonderful film, he shrugged and said that working for Doug with all that money made *Robin Hood* the easiest job he'd ever tackled. Dwan's showmanship was extraordinary. He confided to me that Sidney Kent, the head of Paramount's sales department, had been instrumental in purchasing the magazine story, *Manhandled*, and that he considered it the most saleable property Paramount owned. "That won't exactly hurt us," Allan said with a grin. I agreed that Kent's commercial instincts were sound. Although the original was no literary masterpiece, its heroine's appeal led so many men to make a play for her that when her boyfriend caught one of them pawing her, he accused her of being manhandled. In addition to Kent's belief in the story, Dwan's star would be Gloria Swanson.

At twenty-five, Miss Swanson was unquestionably the paramount glamour girl of the silver screen. Draped in seductive gowns in a series of C.B. DeMille's box office bonanzas, she had become world famous as a *femme fatale*. I was soon privileged to discover other, less publicized qualities in this remarkable young woman. Miss Swanson had just finished a difficult picture. She suggested that she would appreciate a brief vacation at Miami Beach, and added that if Allan Dwan and his writer went along, the spade work on a treatment of *Manhandled* could begin. Paramount said yes. Yes, indeed. Those were the days!

I met Gloria at the Pennsylvania Station just before we took off for Florida. She was much smaller than I had expected, quietly dressed in a smart suit, and wore dark glasses. She couldn't have been friendlier or more gracious. Her companion was Jean Easton. I'd been told that Jean had been recently engaged to advise Gloria about the kind of New Yorkers she should be seen with. A young publisher who had come to see the star off was one of the new "right people" added to Gloria's calling list by Jean Easton.

Shortly after the train pulled out, we were invited to Miss Swanson's drawing room. She had taken off the dark glasses which revealed a glint of unholy mischief in her wonderful eyes. So here I was, en route to Miami with Allan Dwan, Jean Easton, and the star of stars. None of them said a word about *Manhandled*. I was thinking hard. What would be the wisest role for me to play during this combination holiday and story conference? Dwan told an amusing anecdote and told it well. I muttered a small pleasantry. La Swanson giggled and nudged Jean Easton. "That one's a character," she said. That would be it. My safest bet was comedy, which would avoid anything that could offend the triumvirate of judges who would pass sentence on me. I'd be the clown—the court jester. I also made a mental note to get into Jean Easton's good graces and drop the names of a few distinguished Yale graduates. I figured that ladies who live on Snob Hill shouldn't throw names around without having to catch a few. I was definitely on a tightrope.

In Miami, my luck held. Someone banged and rattled the garbage cans below Gloria's window at four in the morning. She got very little sleep. After breakfast, she announced that we were going to Havana. We went.

In those days, the Sevilla Biltmore was only a few months old and was a luxury spot designed to pamper rich Americans, pleasure bent. We blessed whoever had rattled those Miami garbage cans. None of us had ever been outside the United States. To hear people speaking a foreign language and the night cries and songs of street vendors was an exciting experience. The Cubans were all Swanson fans. Scions of the best families guided our sightseeing. At one party the guests danced the rhumba. Gloria took it like a duck to aspic. When she dined in public with the caballeros, Gloria saw to it that Allan, Jean, and I were close at hand. Allan Dwan and I managed to squeeze in a few story sessions, but our attempts to organize our yarn didn't get very far. Allan pointed out that we needed a fresh type of story construction. I agreed, but I also felt that the treatment would have to dig much deeper into the characters of the girl and the boy than the author had done. I didn't mention this to Allan because my ideas were still pretty chaotic.

One morning, Jean Easton and I were picking up our mail. Jean was running over Miss Swanson's letters when she uttered a shocked, "Oh!" I turned to her. She was blushing. "This is dreadful!" she said and handed me the letter so that I could see how dreadful it was and share the vicarious kick she was obviously getting. The note turned out to be an "indecent" proposal to our star. It was corn on the Cuban cob and concluded with a plea to say yes by wearing a rose when she appeared in the lobby that evening. Later Jean told me that Miss Swanson was deeply distressed by the letter. I begged her to tell Gloria to forget the whole thing—it might happen to anyone in her position.

After lunch I paid a call on Miss Swanson with the vague idea of clowning around and getting her mind off the unpleasant incident. She was toying with her food and received me with chilly formality. A few moments later she picked up her tray and vanished into her bedroom. Completely bowled over and mystified, I turned to Jean and Allan. Gloria's companion gave me a stony stare. "She doesn't think it's a bit funny," she said. "What isn't?" I stammered. Jean's lips tightened. "Gloria thinks you wrote that letter," she said. Allen nodded. I searched their faces. If this was a gag, they were doing a great acting job. What could I say? I made an ignominious exit, muttering that I'd be in my room.

Before long, Allan joined me and confessed that Gloria's act was a rib. I dashed to my typewriter and banged out a quickie. It went something like this: "Oh, my sugar! Wear the enclosed in your pretty ear when you go out tonight. When you return, I will be creepetta up the back stairzianza and come to you!" The "enclosed" was the cap of a Coca-Cola bottle. Allan left with my billet doux and I waited.

Finally the telephone rang. A sultry voice said, "This is Miss Swanson. Your second letter isn't funny either!" Click! That night the trio was going to the casino. Just before they left, I called my tormentor. "This is Frank Tuttle," I said. "If you really believe I wrote that letter, life isn't worth living. BANG!" I hung up.

When they flung open my door I was stretched out on the floor, my shirtfront smeared with ketchup. Gloria stared down at the "corpse." "Still not funny," she said. Strike three. I had to sit up. "We are going to the casino," she said icily. Then a radiant smile appeared, followed by an exaggerated Theda Bara leer. "I'll be back," she hissed. "And if you don't make good—." She sailed out of the room, a triumphant vampire. And she called *me* a character!

We arrived back in New York without the treatment. All we had was a collection of scribbled notes. During our holiday, Paramount's Eastern studio had acquired a new executive producer, William LeBaron. He was an able sophisticate, with a distinguished background. He'd written successful plays and musicals and had served as Cosmopolitan Pictures' chief executive. Dwan and I were scheduled to tell him our story at 11:00, the morning after our return. Allan and I had a hurried council of war. I told the director I had a couple of ideas I'd never discussed with him because they hadn't quite jellied. I said I'd stay up all night and dictate some kind of a treatment. Allan wished me good luck and asked me to meet him at LeBaron's apartment at 10:30.

The idea I'd been "mauling" over was that Gloria should work in a department store, and that her leading man—Tom Moore—would be a garage mechanic. They would be roomers in the same cheap boarding house. I felt that Gloria's fans would welcome her as a down-to-earth working girl after all the clotheshorse roles she'd portrayed. I was confident I could devise a reasonable excuse to dress her up once in the picture. Paramount gave me a bright and experienced secretary and we went to work.

Next morning I showed up at LeBaron's with three quarters of a detailed treatment. Allan began to read his copy. The next few moments were agony until the director grinned at me and said, "This is okay, kid. You know, we can use some of this dialogue for titles." I exhaled. At 11:45, Bill LeBaron was equally enthusiastic. Lady Luck was still with me.

When the shooting started I occasionally wandered down to the set. Dwan had embellished my script with sure-fire directorial touches and Gloria's performance was a joy to watch. She seemed to be having the time of her life portraying a real person. Some of Allan's pieces of business were broad comedy. I thought they were great. Only Jean Easton sniffed at them as crude and vulgar. It always struck me as curious that a certain type of intellectual had that reaction to slapstick. Apparently they have forgotten or don't know that slapstick was the essence of the classic commedia dell'arte, and that in the hands of masters like Chaplin, Keaton, Raymond Griffith, and Mack Sennett, it can be something wonderful.

Manhandled was a smash hit. Even before its release, Gloria made a point of declaring, in front of Paramount's bigwigs, that if I started directing again she would be happy to work with me. I never forgot that, and neither did she. Some time later we made a picture together.

One more word about this great lady. I'm sure she never suspected it, but, like 99.44 percent of the men who knew her, I had a terrific case of Gloria Swanson.

CHAPTER 6

Despite his indifference to things theatrical, my father played the star role in the drama that climaxed in my signing as a director with Paramount. Shortly after the release of *Manhandled*, Lloyd Sheldon tipped me off to the company's recent decision to take on a few writers as directors. Lloyd knew about the pictures I'd directed for the Film Guild and set up an appointment for me to discuss the possibility of a director's contract with Jesse Lasky.

The night before our meeting, I tackled father for advice. A shrewd business man, father came right to the point. What, he asked me, was the highest salary a director could get? I told him I thought one or two of them made $5,000 a week. "Ask Lasky for a thousand," he said. My throat tightened in terror as I pointed out that my salary with the Film Guild had been $200. "Ask for a thousand," he said. "Lasky won't shoot you." For father that ended the matter. That night I didn't sleep a wink.

Jesse Lasky was the best-loved executive in the industry. One of its founders, he was a great showman, a soft-spoken gentleman, always easy to approach and devoted to making of fine motion pictures. A story was current that he had recently tried to persuade George Bernard Shaw to sell Paramount the movie rights to his plays. Lasky had argued that such an outstanding dramatist, philosopher, and artist could reach a new, world-wide audience through the movie medium, and he named a figure. Shaw was reputed to have answered that he feared their differences were insurmountable. "The trouble is," said Shaw, "You're interested in art and I'm interested in money!"

Whether this exchange ever took place or not, certainly Jesse Lasky did everything he could to put me at my ease, but my promise to father to ask for a thousand smackers had me as jittery as the traditional penniless suitor asking for the hand of a millionaire's daughter. After the usual preliminary shadow boxing and Lasky's assurance that if we came to terms he would start my directorial career with Richard Dix or Bebe Daniels, it was he who popped the question. How much? Feeling as though I were about to be caught stealing Lasky's famous cornet, I opened my mouth. What came out was a reflex. "A thousand a week," I said. Lasky whistled. Then a sickening silence. Finally, it came. "We'll start you at $750 with Miss Daniels." The rest of the interview is still a blank. That night when I repeated the unbelievable news to father, he laughed. "I told you he wouldn't shoot you," he said.

Dangerous Money, adapted from a novel, *Clark's Field*, was the vehicle selected by Lloyd Sheldon as the first starring vehicle for Bebe Daniels. Both Lloyd and I agreed that only the basic idea of the novel—a girl born and raised in poverty becomes suddenly rich because the value of the strip of land she has inherited suddenly skyrockets—was pictorial. To create an interesting screenplay would take an exceptionally skilled craftsman. Lloyd suggested the best of the available contract writers to work under our supervision. I agreed that the man he suggested was extremely able, but I felt he was wrong for this story. I begged Lloyd to give me Townsend Martin, with whom I had collaborated on several of the Film Guild pictures. Lloyd was reluctant to engage anyone with Townsend's limited experience, but I finally talked him into having a talk with my candidate. The day following my friendly persuasion, Lloyd had a number of important story conferences, which gave me a chance to discuss an approach to *Dangerous Money* with Townsend.

Aside from his talent, Townsend Martin was a born salesman. Before his interview with Lloyd he read the book and digested the picture possibilities. To overcome Sheldon's fear that he was an amateurish tyro, he wore an extremely conservative business suit and stuffed some pencils into his breast pocket. After the preliminary verbal skirmish, he cut loose with a barrage of ideas. In less than twenty minutes, Lloyd was sold. We went to work.

Just before shooing started, we learned that Miss Daniels' favorite cameraman was unavailable, so I began to run pictures during the lunch hour in the hope of finding a first-rate pinch hitter. The photography of J. Roy Hunt finally struck me as exceptionally good. There was some front office opposition to my using a cameraman who had never worked on the Paramount lot, so I proposed that Hunt make a test of Bebe. This was quickly arranged.

When Roy Hunt showed up, he brought with him a delightful southern drawl and an ingratiating manner. It took him only twenty minutes to shoot the test. When Bebe saw it the next morning, she was enchanted and told Roy she had never looked so well. He not only got the job but was put under contract right after the *Dangerous Money* preview and photographed all the pictures Bebe and I made together.

People often ask me if movie stars are difficult. I tell them that if they are I'm sure there's a good reason for it. I have never worked with a temperamental star, and Bebe Daniels was one of the most cooperative. In case you've forgotten, she started her career with Harold Lloyd when she was in her teens. On the way up to stardom she played a great variety of parts, but she shone with an exceptional brightness in her comedy roles. Aside from the technical tricks she'd learned from Harold Lloyd, she was an instinctive comedienne.

When strangers were watching Bebe work, she loved to bedevil them. While we were shooting at a house under the East River Bridge she put on a wonderful act. Dressed in her tacky outfit as the poor girl, she stumbled around like a moron while we were setting up, then suddenly turned to us and asked if I wished her to use expression three or expression six. I went along with the gag and solemnly declared that I thought expression four suited the scene. She said she'd try to give it to me. I need hardly add that she played the scene beautifully. Sometimes directing can be a rugged job, but working with Bebe Daniels was a joy.

Her leading man was Tom Moore, who belonged to a distinguished acting family. His brothers, Owen and Matt, were both fine actors. At college, where I had first seen Tom on the screen of the New Haven Globe Theatre, we were all impressed by the way he dressed. Most of the male movie stars in 1915 sported some astonishing haberdashery, but Tom Moore dressed in the Brooks Brothers' outfits worn by the Ivy Leaguers of that period. He was an outstanding actor of the natural school. What particularly struck me about his work was that he seemed to be completely unaware of the camera. Even in a close-up he would suddenly turn his back or step out of his marks to make a point. And he was a delightful person to be with.

One sequence of *Dangerous Money* took the young heiress to Lake Como, where she was wooed by an impecunious young Italian nobleman, played by William Powell. Our Lake Como mansion was the Benedict Estate in Greenwich, Connecticut—a great personal convenience to me because I lived there. At high tide the estate was architecturally perfect as a Como villa. We had found a close shot of an Italian boatman rowing and speaking to his off-scene passenger, the actual Como scenery behind the Italian. The grips built a replica of the real rowboat and I photographed Tom Moore in the stern of the craft, apparently answering the Italian oarsman.

One weekend some friends of mine, the Morton Nichols, invited Bill Powell and me for dinner. Ordinarily Bill had a justifiable dislike for such occasions, which he described as "come and watch the actors eat" affairs; but I had assured him that Tim and Ethel Nichols weren't that kind of people, so he accepted. The Nichols' cook was an artist. After the fish course, Bill arose, wine glass in hand, and turned to his hostess with an air of gracious solemnity. "I should like to propose a toast," he said, "to the mother of this fish." I have always suspected that this was the beginning of the Powell-Tuttle lifetime friendship.

CHAPTER 7

The surprise package that came with Bebe Daniels' next starring picture, *Miss Bluebeard*, was the top-hat comedian, Raymond Griffith. Ray had been a gag writer for Mack Sennett and had played a smiling killer in director Mickey Neilan's picture, *Fools First*. He first caught the public's fancy as a brilliant comic in William DeMille's *Changing Husbands*.

Ray spoke in a hoarse whisper. The loss of his voice was usually attributed to his shouting in a stage melodrama. However, his onetime roommate, Scoop Conlon, is my authority for stating that the injury to Ray's vocal chords was the result of childhood diphtheria. Scoop was a close friend of mine and of directors George Stevens, Howard Hawks, Lewis Milestone, and George Marshall, whose careers and pictures he publicized until he died.

In any case, working with Ray was a course in the art of slapstick. Aside from his talent and experience, Ray's humor was not confined to the visual comedy he devised for himself. Several years after *Miss Bluebeard*, when he was a full-fledged Paramount star, I recall his returning from an unsuccessful attempt to get a substantial raise from the front office. His salary at the time was in the neighborhood of $3,000 a week. He growled at me hoarsely, "Sons of bitches! They won't give a guy a living wage!"

Ray had just arrived from Hollywood when I met him on one of our sets. The character he was to play was the Honorable Bertie Bird, created in the stage production by Eric Blore. Bebe's role was that of a French actress—played by Irene Bordoni on Broadway—who had been married by the mayor of an obscure French town to an American she'd met on the train. To impress the actress this young tourist had said he was Larry Charters, a popular composer. They had both assumed that the mayor, who was also the proprietor of the town's hotel, was entering their names in the register when he was actually marrying them.

Later the couple barged into Charters' apartment in London to explain to the composer that he has been married to Bebe by proxy. The Bertie Bird character was what Ray called a "bob-in," that is, a comic who sporadically showed up to add to the farcical situations devised by playwright Avery Hopwood.

After a few pleasantries and the inevitable explanation of his hoarseness, Ray asked me to tell him the story. He hadn't read the script. We were on the set that represented Larry Charters' flat. When I came to Bertie Bird's introduction, Ray jumped up and gave me an engaging smile. "I'm over here," he whispered, "taking a nap on this couch. It'll be a running gag. All through the picture I'll be trying to catch up on my sleep!" I saw that this had possibilities and agreed.

When the shooting started, we soon discovered Ray's amazing talent for adlibbing. I believe one example deserves a detailed resume. Townsend and I had written a short bit where Bertie, having fled the redecorating which was going on in his own diggings, wanders into Charters' flat to get a night's sleep. When he opens a bedroom door, he discovers Bebe asleep. Bertie reacts and flees. The day before we were to shoot this brief nothing, Ray suggested that we take a look at the bedroom set. The door through which Bertie was to make his entrance was in the rear wall, and there were doors in the right and left side walls. Ray studied the layout for all of one minute. Then he acted out the routine he'd been cooking up. The right-hand door would lead to a bathroom, the door in the opposite wall to a dressing room.

The scene would open with the nightgowned Bebe taking toilet articles from her bag into the bathroom. At the exact moment of her exit, Ray would appear in the center door, move quickly to the bed, feel its alluring softness, select a pair of his host's pajamas from a chest of drawers and vanish happily into the dressing room; whereupon Bebe would reappear and collect another item from her bag. These near-misses would continue until Bebe and Ray actually got into the huge bed from opposite sides, without either of them knowing there was anyone else in the room.

Until this moment the scene would be played without a cut. The next setup would be a close shot of the two in bed, Ray dozing off to sleep and Bebe gradually becoming conscious that she was not alone. Slowly turning she would see Ray's head and scream. Robert Frazer, as Larry

Charters, and Kenneth MacKenna, as Bebe's second "husband," would dash in and find the hysterical Bebe pointing to Ray, who was now in the process of crawling under his pillow—a somewhat inadequate hiding place. The sequence would end with the two men grabbing the terrified offender and giving him the bum's rush.

There is an interesting footnote to the above.

Came the talkies and Paramount did a remake of *Miss Bluebeard*, retitling it *Her Wedding Night*. In the new version, the new star was Clara Bow, and Charlie Ruggles played the Griffith part. I ran the old silent picture for Charlie Ruggles and asked him how he'd like to change the playing of the role. The veteran stage and screen comedian paid Ray Griffith the highest compliment one actor could pay another. "I won't change a gesture," he said. And he didn't.

Ray and I became fast friends. I was privileged to direct his last silent picture for Paramount, which was shot in Hollywood. I had the added enjoyment of working on the screenplay with Ray, an invaluable experience which had a profound effect upon my comedy equipment.

As those TV announcers say, let's pause here for station identification. This is Frank Tuttle, about to meander again. It seems to me that the writer of an autobiography can never be wholly detached from his beginnings nor his prejudices. Even if he is keenly conscious of them and tries to avoid their promptings, they are bound to crop up in the unconscious background of his anecdotage and his opinions.

Perhaps one of the most important facts about me that I've neglected to mention is that I've never been desperately poor nor close to starvation. Ring Lardner described my situation perfectly when he said about himself that he'd known what it was to be hungry but had always walked right into a restaurant. With me it was often the automat, but in the worse moments of distress there has always been someone to turn to. Undoubtedly this accounts for my ability to bound up quickly when I've been floored by adversity; and a sense of guilt about my own good luck probably explains my wanting to help anyone less fortunate than I. Another characteristic is my need to be liked—a trait which can become a weakness unless you keep telling yourself that anyone worth his salt should have a few enemies he can be proud of.

I also believe that it was a break for me that I started directing in the silent era. I still think that what people say on the screen is less effective than what they do. You'll remember that Austin Strong, speaking about the theatre, had this point of view. Certainly action and pieces of business were the dominant factors in the silent days. On the other hand, with a few exceptions, ideas were scanty. Screen writers of the stature of Ibsen or Shaw never appeared in this period. But directors did learn to tell a story with a camera, and when pictures began to talk the outstanding directors of the new vocal phase for the most part were men experienced in the old techniques.

The directors who were schooled in the methods of the silents preferred to illustrate the theme of a story in terms of action rather than to talk about it. When the change came, I believe they regarded dialogue as a substitute for the spoken title. I'm sure they felt that it was an improvement, compared to a technique which involved the sudden appearance of white lettering on a black surface and the disappearance of the actors.

The list of winners of the Academy Award for direction since the element of talking was introduced features a large percentage of graduates from the schools of the silent era. Apparently many of the recruits from the theatre are also convinced that the audience eye is more important than its ear.

CHAPTER 8

The Manicure Girl, my next picture with Bebe Daniels, was pretty pallid compared to our first two ventures together, largely, it seems to me now, because it was a sentimental triangle story in which the heroine became involved with a man who she eventually discovered was married. To keep its whiskers from showing, this antique situation takes the kind of persuasive writing with which Noel Coward later endowed *Brief Encounter*. Despite sensitive performances by Bebe, Hale Hamilton, and Charlotte Walker, who played Hamilton's wife, the vehicle creaked. However, the New York Paramount casting department did have the same access to theatre talent that the British studios have to their stage greats. For a short but amusing character bit in *The Manicure Girl*, for example, they secured the services of Victor Moore, just before he became the toast of Broadway for his delightful performance as Vice-President Throttlebottom in *Of Thee I Sing*. Luckily for me and my star, audiences were beginning to flock to Bebe Daniels' pictures, so the box office rang up another moneymaker for Paramount.

We were happier with our fourth effort, *Lovers in Quarantine*, in which the popular Harrison Ford appeared as Bebe's leading man and Alfred Lunt played a secondary role. Lynn Fontanne paid us a visit on one of our locations, and our lunch hour was a joy listening to their witty show talk.

Incidentally, my favorite anecdote about actors, true or apocryphal, involves the Lunts. While they were in Hollywood making a picture version of *The Guardsman*, the assistant director knocked on their dressing room door after the second day's shooing and told them that the rushes of the first day's work were ready for them to look at. Mr. Lunt pleaded stage fright and begged his wife to report back to him after she'd seen what he feared would be a death blow to his ego. When she returned, she was on the verge of tears despite the fact that Alfred, she declared, was a born picture actor. His performance was magnificent and, except for a few shots in which he seemed to have no eyebrows, his appearance was equally impressive. As for herself—WELL!! She overacted, she made faces, and she looked like one of the witches in *Macbeth*. She would never see another rush. "But, Alfred," she concluded, "You are *divine*!" Mr. Lunt was not happy. He turned to his mirror. Finally he spoke. "No eyebrows!" he said.

Lovers in Quarantine was based on a successful play. The movie adaptation took us to Bermuda. Roy Hunt did a brilliant job with the beauties of that picturesque British possession. The picture did very well indeed at the box office.

Following the pictures with Bebe, I was assigned to direct Richard Dix. Richard had been recruited from the theatre and had won stardom in a varied type of characterizations. Our association was in the field of comedy-melodrama. Unlike some of the other serious actors of the period, he had a flair for farce. He enjoyed making himself ridiculous if the script called for it. He used to refer to himself as a $40 a week actor who'd been lucky.

Which makes a perfect transition to the picture we did together— *Lucky Devil*. The story climaxed in a cross-country automobile race, complete with thrills, spills, and gags. Richard's leading lady was Esther Ralston, beautiful and a real trouper. Her aunt was played by Edna May Oliver, the noted character actress. Edna May's reactions to calamity were so ribtickling that Esther and Richard were constantly on the verge of breaking up when her pursed lips and baleful eyes were accompanied by her famous sniff. Usually, at the end of one of her scenes, my shouted "Cut!" was followed by a chorus of guffaws from all of us.

The location for the automobile race was Lakewood, New Jersey. A second unit director was in charge of shooting the skids and hair-raising misses with doubles. He did a magnificent job. Later, after we had run a rough cut of *Lucky Devil*, he asked me if I could see my way to giving him some kind of credit. I told him I'd recommend to William LeBaron that the following should be added to the main title: "Race directed by GREGORY LA CAVA." Gregory was delighted and somewhat astonished, but I told him the title credit was a simple statement of fact. A few months after this, Greg became a full-fledged director, and before he died several years ago, he directed scores of notable movies, among them, the outstanding comedy with Bill Powell and Carole Lombard, *My Man Godfrey*.

At this point it occurs to me that some of you may be asking yourselves what people ask Hugh Downs about Jack Paar, "What's he really like?" When I started scribbling I somehow assumed that when I'd gone a ways, my character would have pretty much revealed itself—as much, at least, most people's characters become apparent after you've been with them for awhile. Naturally, most autobiographers instinctively conceal their faults and dress themselves up for their readers, so it might be a good idea if I gave you a brief and truthful picture of me—if indeed we are ever capable of seeing ourselves "as *others* see us." Okay.

As I stand on the bathroom scale, I weigh 162 pounds and I'm six feet one and a half. I have most of my hair and it and my mustache are nearly white. My eyebrows are grey and brown caterpillars. I am nearsighted and wear bone-rimmed glasses.

Like most New Yorkers, I don't pronounce the "r" in Yorker. I say New Yalk—to rhyme with talk and walk. I'm a good listener and try to form my opinions slowly, although I'm a sucker for clever salesmen, particularly if they're pretty girls. I like most people and when I don't, I avoid them because I hate fights.

Even when writing and directing jobs are extremely difficult and tough problems arise I enjoy the work and will knock myself out trying to get it right. During the preparatory period, I proceed with considerable caution, but once we really get going I know what I want and move quickly and with conviction.

Politically I started as a conservative, then moved gradually to the left until I was abruptly disillusioned. Today I am a moderate progressive whose ideal American is a man like Carl Sandburg. My credo is simple. Like Mahatma Gandhi, I believe that "Truth is God," and, like Tom Paine, "To do good is my religion."

The American Venus was dreamed up by Paramount's exploitation boys to capitalize on the notoriety attained by the Atlantic City beauty contests. The cast included Esther Ralston, Larry Gray, Louise Brooks, Edna May Oliver, and Ford Sterling, who had departed from the style he had immortalized as chief of the Keystone Kops and appeared in the movie version of George Kelly's *The Showoff*.

Writer Townsend Martin and I were both afraid that a picture about bathing beauties might be criticized as cheap, so we decided to kid the subject. Roy Hunt was assigned to photograph it.

I shall never forget the reaction of the Atlantic City crowds when Esther Ralston appeared among the real contestants in the boardwalk parade. This sequence was hot in Technicolor. Esther had always been associated with the type of part which accented her ethereal qualities. Her fans had never been privileged to get a good look at her figure, which was spectacular. Perhaps it can best be described as a pre-Marilyn Monroe doctrine. The spectators didn't whistle. They couldn't. Their mouths were wide open.

Louise Brooks played the light-comedy heavy among the contestants. Louise was a graduate, *magna cum laude*, of the Ziegfeld Follies. She had an impish sense of humor. In her bathing suit, a straw skimmer cocked over one eye, she did a wonderful job in a scene with Ford Sterling, who played one of the judges of the contest. Ford's myopic ball and chain was Edna May Oliver. She interrupted a tête-à-tête between her spouse and Louise Brooks, who had showed up to impress the judge with her qualifications. Ford outwitted his nearsighted wife by going into a Chinese magician routine—hiding his visitor behind a voluminous shawl until she could escape, while Edna May was searching for her glasses.

Ford contributed a funny piece of business to another actor. In this sequence our hero's car had been demolished in an accident en route to Atlantic City. A society drunk, in high hat and tails, had given Larry Gray a lift. At one point in the drunk's erratic driving, he thought he recognized a tramp who had stolen his wallet. A chase ensued around two haystacks. Ford suggested that the audience might laugh if each of the men suddenly began to run around a separate haystack. He was right. They howled. And *The American Venus* was a hit.

Adolphe Menjou was a joy to work with. Aside from his talent, he was meticulously conscientious. If his morning call was for 9:00, he was ready to go several minutes before that. He would willingly replace his stand-in to give the cameraman a chance to improve his lighting. He used to wink at his alter ego and say, "Get out of there! You'll get my job."

Unlike many actors, Menjou attributed a large part of his success to luck. He told everyone that Chaplin's decision to use him in *A Woman of Paris* was responsible for his rise to stardom. He admired the talent of other good actors. He ballyhooed the ability of several of the White Russians who were a small but gifted segment of the Hollywood film colony.

I remember an anecdote about one Russian actor. I'll call him "Passky." He spoke almost no English and had been introduced to the casting departments of all the big studios by a bilingual Russian friend who left Passky's card with his telephone number in all the casting offices. Naturally Passky could only work as an extra, but he was flat broke and happy to pick up what he could while he was learning English. Now it happens that the big studios are here, there, and somewhere else. If his telephone rang, the Russian quickly said, "Passky!" The man in the casting office rattled off a message to be on stage number something or other at so-and-so studio the next morning at 8:00. Passky said, "Sank you," and hung up. Nine times out of ten, his terrified ear heard and his brain understood nothing except that he was to be at some studio at 8:00. The next morning he rattled in his jalopy to all the studios, starting at 7:30, until someone looked at his card and pointed out the set. The poor man must have often covered miles and miles getting to his job.

The subtle suavity of Adolphe Menjou's characterizations has an interesting sidelight. In real life he is as direct, forceful, and blunt as he is deft and polished on the screen. If he has an opinion, he comes right out with it, particularly where money is concerned. In the early days he had been a unit manager and had learned a tough lesson or two about the handling of funds; but his first love was acting, and, luckily for American moving pictures, he got the break that gave him his chance to develop and display his fine talent.

Our first picture together was *A Kiss in the Dark*, based on the Lonsdale play, *Aren't We All?* Once again, Townsend Martin wrote the screenplay and, as had been the case with *Dangerous Money*, the original was pretty skimpy in cinematic material and ideas. Townsend did his usual expert job, praise be, and we were finally ready to go with a script, which L Baron and Sheldon thoroughly approved.

The cast included Aileen Pringle and Kenneth MacKenna, who had become a close friend of mine since his screen debut in *Miss Bluebeard*. Pringie, as Adolphe's leading lady was known to her friends, was what Gloria Swanson had called me—"a character." Her figure was a delight to the ladies who designed her wardrobe and her sly remarks about people were a delight to me. Occasionally her remarks were censorable—but discreetly so. I remember a platitudinous bore delivering an endless and pointless harangue to Pringie and a group of her friends. When the obnoxious jerk had finally left, we turned to Aileen hopefully. She smiled sweetly and murmured, "Hmm. The bastard type!" I once attended a dinner party she gave for fourteen people. Pringie was the only woman present. The rest of us had the time of our lives. So did our heavenly hostess.

I have already mentioned that colorful locations within striking distance of New York were hard to find. With this in mind, plus my happy memories of the place, I suggested to Townsend that Havana would be an ideal locale for several of the outdoor sequences in *A Kiss in the Dark*. He leaped at the idea, particularly since in those days the writer frequently went along with the troupe.

Our timing was perfect. America was still in the midst of *The Dry Decade,* as Charles Merz dubbed prohibition in his book with that title. We arrived in Havana in time for the Sevilla Biltmore's New Year's Eve party and took the next day off as a holiday, during which we could recuperate before the shooting started. We were grateful to Paramount for the break and went to work in fine fettle.

Just as they had when Swanson and Dwan had invaded Havana, the Cuban caballeros attached themselves to the company and became the gallant escorts of Pringie when she wasn't working. I must hasten to add that Aileen's gadding about a bit was icing on her Cuban cake. Picture people work hard. The players are up at the crack to be made up and transported to the location where they're working. After lunch they work as long as the light lasts. Evenings, the staff plans the next day's work. No one plays unless he's free the next day. Even in the gala surroundings of Havana, we finished our job a day ahead of schedule and shot a scene with Moro Castle in the background as we sailed out of Havana Harbor. Yes, we worked like hell and we thoroughly enjoyed ourselves. Only in Puritan America, I think, would the two facts seem incongruous. Our still camera crew shot plenty of pictures of the interiors adjoining the exteriors we'd shot, so that it was easy to match the sets constructed in Astoria with the Cuban locations. At this time there was no actor's guild, so I played a tiny bit in Havana—a young Cuban—so that the character could walk into our Long Island set without Paramount having to pay for transporting a native actor.

The studio heads were pleased with the rushes we brought back with us, and we wound up the shooting in a few weeks after our return. *A Kiss in the Dark* was well received by the public and the critics.

CHAPTER 9

My next assignment took me to the West Coast, which I'd never seen. In 1925, Hollywood had taken root and developed into the moving picture capital of the world. It was an eccentric community in the sense that it was devoted almost exclusively to making movies. Back East, when you left the Astoria studio, you returned to anonymity in New York or its environs. Weekends you frequently saw no one connected with your vocation. The topics of conversation varied according to your taste and the taste of your friends. In my case, books and the current Broadway plays were the major subjects discussed. In Hollywood people talked shop almost exclusively. However, this community's preoccupation with picture making had its advantages. If you wanted a midget, a lion, or an albino who could act, he was available; and when you weren't working, a variety of places where you could relax were near at hand. Even by train, New York was less than a week away.

At first Hollywood struck me as an enigma. It seemed to be *nouveau riche*, garish, the tinsel town I had more or less expected to find. It was only after I'd gone back to New York and made a second trip to Hollywood that its true character came into view, and I began to like it. Of course those Hollywood parties which Bill Powell used to describe as affairs where the guests entered in the order of their salaries did exist. On the other hand, there were other gatherings of just a few people where close friends talked about all manner of things—and with humor and intelligence. The truth was that if you made the effort you could find pretty much the kind of companionship you wanted to find. I'm convinced that a good deal of the sneering at Hollywood you heard in those days had its basis in ignorance and perhaps a touch of envy.

One aspect of Hollywood during the jazz age which calls for comment is its reputation for wild parties and drunken orgies. I'm tempted to

A cartoon drawn by Frank Tuttle en route to California.

dismiss the whole subject by saying that I saw nothing in Hollywood which I hadn't already seen in New York's suburbia. It is true, of course, that prohibition had brought with it the hip flask, flaming youth, and whoopee, but this was a national phenomenon. The essential difference between Hollywood and Peoria was that Hollywood was news. It got the headlines and the spotlight. Actually the picture of the film capital as the Sodom and Gomorrah of the twenties was a distorted caricature. By and large the citizens of "Filmlandia" were as hardworking and respectable as their counterparts anywhere in the United States; and whatever transgressions they were guilty of were common to the whole American scene. Certainly there could be no more striking example of this than the star of the picture which took us to Hollywood.

Eddie Cantor was as solid a citizen as you could find anywhere. His wife, Ida, and the Cantor girls were, in fact, a symbol of American family life. They *were* the "Joneses" except that in this case, Mr. Jones was a great comic. In Beverly Hills, we had bungalows at the same hotel, and I saw a great deal of these warm and wonderful people during the filming of *Kid Boots*.

Under Lloyd Sheldon's able supervision, Townsend Martin and I had done a careful job on the screenplay. To make a silent movie out of a Broadway musical isn't easy. Without the decorative Ziegfeld beauties, musical numbers, and spoken jokes to fill in where the story lags, the screenplay has to supply situations and gags that will photograph. The reward for our hard work came when Eddie Cantor read the finished script. "A broom could play my part," he said.

Paramount gave us a fine cast. Eddie's leading lady was Clara Bow, now world famous as the "It Girl." The romantic leads were Larry Gray and Billie Dove, the reigning beauty of that era.

It is extremely difficult to describe a silent comedy routine, but I'll try to give you a picture of one of the brief bits which had aroused Eddie's enthusiasm. Clara has had a tiff with Eddie, so he tries to make her jealous. They are dining separately in a restaurant which is almost empty. Near Eddie's table is a screen. He pulls it close, slips his left arm out of his coat, rolls up his sleeve and pats his arm with powdered sugar. The action which follows is played from Clara's point of view. Eddie's hand and powdered arm appear from behind the screen. The "girl's" fingers caress Eddie's cheek and chuck him under the chin. He reacts coyly and kisses the fluttering hand. His flirtation with himself continues until Clara is fit to be tied. Incidentally, Eddie was wrong. No broom could have evoked the laughter that rewarded his performance of this dual role. The topper to the gag came when Eddie hurried to Clara's table, explained his trick, returned to his own table and pulled back the screen. Unhappily for Eddie, his action revealed a sexy blonde who had seated herself while Eddie was convincing Clara of his innocence. No? Ah, well. I guess you had to be there.

The critics hailed Eddie Cantor's first appearance on the screen as a triumph. One of them headlined his review with, "VERY GOOD EDDIE!"

Before my return to New York after *Kid Boots* had been edited and previewed, Eddie and I adlibbed an evening of nonsense at our hotel for a few of our friends. Among our guests was Mary Astor, now a seasoned performer and lovelier to look at than ever. From his vast backlog of blackouts, Eddie came up with a dozen or so to perform with Mary and me. A couple of them are worth recalling here to give you a rough idea of one Hollywood party of 1925.

In one blackout Mary and I came on talking about a family problem involving our small son, Eddie. His beloved dog, Paddy, had just died and I declared that I couldn't face Eddie's grief when he learned of the tragedy and walked off. Now Eddie appeared, stirring something in a large bowl. In the ickiest kind of baby talk, he announced that he was mixing a delicious tidbit for Paddy. Mary put her arm around him and whispered that Paddy was dead. Eddie gurgled happily and went right on with his stirring. Mary lifted his chin. "You must stop that, Eddie dear," she said. "*Paddy is dead!*" Eddie burst into tears. "But Eddie," Mary said soothingly, "I just told you." Eddie's sobbing became a wail. "I thought you said *daddy*," he said.

The other one was a quickie. Eddie came on and explained that he was an impoverished father, trying to save himself and his daughter, Mary, from the poorhouse. He persuaded her to lie down in the street, in the hope that a rich stranger would happen by, see his beautiful child, obviously dying of starvation, and offer them help. End of exposition. Enter the stranger—me. I saw the recumbent figure, knelt, and lifted her head. "What a beautiful girl," I said, "and drunk!" Blackout! Ah, me. Those Hollywood orgies!

Like many directors, I secretly love to act and, as I've told you, I'd done quite a bit of it at college and with the Comedy Club. Talking about Eddie's blackouts reminded me of my one professional acting appearance, which happened several years later.

I had written a sketch for one of the anniversary numbers of *The Hollywood Reporter* and titled it *Keep It Clean*. It had a satiric angle, kidding the current self-imposed censorship in the industry. A fictitious Elizabethan producer, Somerset, has hired Francis Bacon to clean up the blue situations in Shakespeare's *Hamlet*. In the presence of the great playwright, Somerset's pretty secretary takes down the "improvements." They are, of course, monstrous and ruinous to the play and its author's sensitivity. After several futile protests, Shakespeare takes poison and drops dead. Somerset's reaction is true to type. He shouts to the secretary, "Shakespeare's name off the payroll—as of *now!*" Curtain.

Some friends of mine who had read the sketch were putting on a charity affair. They thought that *Keep It Clean* would supply the comedy needed for their program and asked me to stage it for them. Instead I persuaded Roland Young—about whom you'll hear more later—to take over this chore. I wanted to play Somerset. Roland agreed and directed the sketch with the following cast.

William Shakespeare	Charles Arnt
Francis Bacon	Colin Tapley
Somerset	Frank Tuttle
His Secretary	*Katherine DeMille
	*(later Mrs. Anthony Quinn)

Simultaneously with the charity show, a revival of vaudeville was running at the Wilshire-Ebell Theatre. Its producer showed up at our performance and made us an offer to pay us for an appearance the following week. We accepted and we had a ball. One interesting additional fact. The audience which had paid for its tickets to see a professional show greeted us with bigger and louder laughs than the charity audience.

Shortly after the *Kid Boots* preview, a life insurance test indicated that I might be a diabetic. My doctor made a thorough examination and confirmed this. Since I was returning to New York, he suggested that I contact the leading specialist in this field back there. He was Dr. Frederick Allen, whose definition of diabetes is still quoted in the textbooks, and whose "Physiatric Institute" was then in Morristown, New Jersey. I took my doctor's advice and, after a couple of weeks stay at the Institute, I was put on a permanent insulin and weighed food diet routine. That was in 1925, and I've been a controlled diabetic ever since.

I believe it was one of the Mayo brothers who said that certain ailments are a great safeguard. They force you to take care of yourself so that your chances of living to a ripe old age are usually greater than those of the normal, overindulgent human. In my case, this has certainly been true. At sixty-eight, I am paunchless and tremendously active. I've directed close to a hundred movies and finished over eighty percent of them ahead of schedule. In fact, I have an idiotic conviction that I'm going to live forever. Back to Methuselah!

As I bat out this rambling account of movie happenings and people, it occurs to me that what I've written so far may be giving the impression that I like practically everyone. This could dilute the critical value of my opinions. In a way, it's true. I do like most people, but the great majority of those I've worked with have been likeable. That's the simple fact. And don't worry. When someone who rubbed me the wrong way turns up in this autobiography, I'll say so and I'll tell you why. *There's* a sneaky trick to lure you into reading further!

The personality I met on my return trip to New York was, and still is, one of my all-time favorites. Evelyn Brent was to play the feminine lead in *Love 'Em and Leave 'Em*, which was based on John V.A. Weaver's play of that name. Miss Brent had a drawing room in the car next to mine. At that time she was married to Bernard Fineman, one of Paramount's producers. I dropped by and introduced myself. This was in the days before air conditioning, and Miss Brent was doing her best to fight off the heat with an electric fan. She was a slender, dark-haired young lady, with a fine forehead and wonderful, intelligent eyes. I had admired her sensitive performances with Clive Brook and George Bancroft. We sweltered through the conventional conversational gambits, then, as we got to know one another, I discovered that she was a warm and wonderful person. When I left, I felt that working with her would be a stimulating experience.

Love 'Em and Leave 'Em preceded *My Sister Eileen* by several years, but it told the same basic story of a working girl, Evelyn Brent, who has to mother her younger sister. In *Love 'Em and Leave 'Em*, the kid sister was a spoiled brat who even tries to steal her sister's boyfriend, played by Larry Gray. Townsend Martin's screenplay needed only a *soupçon* of polishing, and we were ready to go in less than two weeks after my return to Astoria. Louise Brooks was cast as the younger sister, and we were lucky enough to get Osgood Perkins, whom I hadn't seen since the Film Guild days, for a role which called for his playing most of his scenes with Betty Brent. I had persuaded Os, whose stage career was just beginning, that a return to the screen in a Paramount picture would be super for us both. Working with him was like conducting a concerto with Horowitz at the keyboard. Mal St. Clair, one of Jesse Lasky's prize directors, wandered over to our set one day and asked me who the actor was who was chewing on that toothpick. I told him about Osgood and he said, "He's great. I hope I can find a part for him."

On the morning we started shooting, I was astonished to find that Esther Ralston had replaced Evelyn Brent. Let me quickly add that Esther had nothing to do with the switch, which had originated in the front office for some reason I have never been able to fathom. Perhaps the higher ups were trying to capitalize on a recent Ralston hit. In any case, it was a real contretemps. Fond as I was of Esther, I couldn't help feeling that Evelyn Brent's qualities and appearance suited the part perfectly. I did the best I could to readjust myself to the change. Esther was her usual cooperative self and we finished the day's work with only a slight feeling of tension.

Next morning, Evelyn Brent walked onto the set. The powers that be had switched the switch. I never found out the "whys and wherefores" of this one either. My guess was that Betty's husband, Bernie Fineman, had heard the news in Hollywood and raised long-distance hell.

Be that as it may, I found myself in a most embarrassing spot that called for tact plus. And I was furious at the thick skins responsible for the dilemma. What kind of people, I thought, would assign a role to an actress because she is talented and sensitive and then slap her face by yanking her out of the part. Russ Mathews, my assistant and I did our darnedest to salve our star's *amour propre* and make our sympathy and understanding obvious. Like us, Osgood had fallen for Betty like a ton of brick-a-brac and she reciprocated. After the picture had really begun to swing, Betty told me that if all of us had hadn't been so considerate she would have quit the show. Naturally none of this affected her performance, which she was exceptionally convincing.

Directors try to avoid clichés in an actor's reaction to a more or less conventional situation, or at least to make the reaction completely honest. At one point in our story, the older sister suddenly discovers the brat kissing her boyfriend. I had already decided to shoot Evelyn's reaction through the narrow opening of the hinged side of a bedroom door, but I hadn't figured

The music cue sheet for *Blind Alleys*, Tuttle's 1927 film starring Thomas Meighan, with Evelyn Brent, Greta Nissen, Hugh Miller, Thomas Chalmers, and Tammany Young.

the right piece of business for Betty. I told her what was troubling me and we both began to puzzle over the right move. Betty's concentration caused her to press her cheeks with both hands. "That's it," I said. So when we took the shot, that's what she did and it worked perfectly.

Louise Brooks had lost none of that special quality, which had contributed so much to the success of *The American Venus*. One of her scenes in *Love 'Em and Leave 'Em* called for her dancing the Black Bottom. Next day we saw the rushes together. "I should have stuck to my dancing," she said. It was indeed a high moment, but I quickly reassured her that her offbeat elfin personality was the real thing.

At coffee break time, Os Perkins and I talked about everything imaginable with Evelyn Brent. You usually get to know your leading players and what makes them tick before you've finished directing a picture. The more I knew Betty the more I admired her. I loved working with her and I loved her—but who didn't? Less than a year after *Love 'Em and Leave 'Em* was previewed, I returned to Hollywood. I still treasure the photograph Evelyn Brent gave me. On it she had written, "Love 'em and leave 'em and send 'em a photo—Betty."

CHAPTER 10

One curious fact about this grab bag of movies and personalities is that the only reference source I've used is a mimeographed biography which includes a list of all the pictures I've directed. When I suddenly realized that a great deal of what I've talked about happened some thirty or forty years ago, I was astonished that I had remembered names and incidents so accurately. The more I thought about this the more I became convinced that the explanation was really quite simple. I'm one of those lucky guys who loves what he's doing and the great majority of those who have worked with him. I imagine the psychology experts would agree with this point. I seem to recall their saying that we shut out the unpleasant from our conscious mind and dwell on the good things.

Raymond Griffith's starring film, *Time to Love*, took me back to Hollywood and, except for occasional returns of the native of New York and an occasional foray to Europe, I've lived there ever since. I've already said that I like California and I've told you why, but there's one feature of Hollywood that I neglected to mention. You can be in the country there without being a suburbanite. Deer and rabbits bounded about the countryside surrounding one of the houses I lived in, yet the studio and the heart of town were only ten minutes away. And it's quiet. You're often asleep by 10:30 P.M. when you're working, and in the summer your slumber isn't assailed by sweltering humidity. I admire the stamina of New Yorkers who stay up until 2:00 A.M. and are on the job at 9:30 the next day, but I don't envy it. If you do have a yen for New York's theatres and nightspots, you can hop a plane and be a town mouse for a week or two, which is just about all I can take. If this be treason, the drinks are on me.

I believe I've mentioned that I learned a lot about visual comedy working on the script of *Time to Love* with Ray, and the actual shooting also contributed to my education in this field. Ray played a famous French duelist who had been forced to challenge Bill Powell to a duel. For rather complicated plot reasons, which I'll spare you from listening to, the two men, whose families had been close friends for years, had secretly arranged to miss one another, but Ray would pretend to fall dead. In the first exchange, Ray's trademark, his high hat, was shot off, obviously, a double cross. Bill must be trying to kill him. Ray hurried forward and protested. Bill's answer was a title written by George Marion, Jr. "I suddenly thought," he explained, "that if I fired into the air, I might kill some harmless bird." Ray accepted the apology, but when Bill winged the hat again, he was furious. Bill was even more apologetic in his protestations of innocence. They prepared to shoot once more.

Now Ray was to pretend to fall, mortally wounded. He called me aside and pointed out a dilemma. If he clutched his side or made any violent move, the audience would laugh because of the horseplay they'd just witnessed. Ray asked me how to prevent this. Of course he knew the answer. I racked my brains, but I couldn't figure it out. Ray smiled. "I do absolutely nothing," he said. "Then I'll start swaying, slowly—and finally, I'll fall." He was absolutely right. At the preview they whopped at the hat bit, but after the third shot, when Ray stood motionless, they stopped laughing.

Another instance of the way the silk hat comedian's mind worked. Later in the story, Ray comes back to see the girl, whom Bill is going to marry, disguised as a ghost, complete with sheet and halo. Bill catches them and starts shooting at Ray, who bounces up and down on a bed, ducking the bullets. When I asked Ray what he planned to do to get out of this cul-de-sac, he replied that he'd reach under the bed, come up with a fire axe, and chase Bill through the assembled wedding guests. I protested that a fire axe under the bed in a French chateau was too far-fetched even for farce. Ray shrugged. "If I come up with it," he said, "it must have been there." Once again he was right. The audience was so enchanted by Bill Powell running for his life from a sheeted maniac with a halo swinging the axe, that their sense of logic went out the window and they howled with delight at the ludicrous picture.

Incidentally, writing comedy titles in the silent days was a job for a highly specialized talent. George Marion, Jr., was one of the best. And when the talkies came he wrote a number of delightful comedies with brilliant dialogue. Ray Griffith's all-time favorite title was concocted by

Johnny Gray, who wrote for Mack Sennett. The situation into which Gray fitted it occurred in one of those down-on-the-farm Sennett classics. The heroine had just confessed that she was pregnant. Her outraged father demanded the name of her seducer. The ravished girl lowered her eyes and whispered, "He came to paint the barn." As Ray pointed out, the unfunny words painted such a graphic picture of what had happened that, Ray told me, audiences used to take a count of four to grasp it and then—BOFF!

The three pictures that followed *Time to Love*, starred Esther Ralston, Richard Dix, and Adolphe Menjou about whose talents and personalities I've already told you. The other films introduced me to three people I'd never worked with before this.

Charles (Buddy) Rogers had made an instant hit in a picture Paramount produced with a group of youngsters whom the Astoria studio had discovered in one of those nation-wide talent searches for prospective future stars. Buddy's outstanding qualities were his youthful good looks and his sincerity. He had something of the winning charm that later characterized Van Johnson when he won the affection of America as "the boy next door." Buddy was a fine athlete and an excellent musician, and he was never content to drift along as a personality. He was a hard worker, eagerly watching and learning from his more experienced colleagues. He gradually became an able and reliable performer.

Florence Vidor was one of the loveliest ladies of the screen with a vast fund of quiet humor. Her performance as a Russian aristocrat in *The Grand Duchess and the Waiter*, in which she co-starred with Adolphe Menjou, was directed by Malcolm St. Clair and won her millions of admirers all over the world. She played with quiet restraint and was graced with a subtle appeal. Recognized everywhere as one of the screen's outstanding personalities and actresses, I was fearful at first that she might be a bit standoffish. On the contrary, she was a delight to work with and we became great friends.

In one of the pictures we did together, a supporting player was Hedda Hopper, to whom I'd been introduced several years before this during the Film Guild days by James Ashmore Creelman. Hedda was a top performer, and between takes she was a sly and delightful raconteuse. While the crew was setting up for the next shot, she would let fly with a barbed comment about someone we all had the misfortune to know which scored a laugh bull's-eye, and reminded me of Aileen Pringle's rapier wit. After giving up the acting profession, Hedda's career has been anything but a step backward, as her thousands of devoted readers can testify. Her newspaper column is syndicated from coast-to-coast.

In one of the *Potash and Perlmutter* plays, the two famous suit and coat manufactures had a fling at "moom pitcha" production—and why not? As Abe Potash said, "Everybody's got two professions. His own and moving pictures." That was certainly true in the silent days when Montague Glass wrote about Potash and Perlmutter. And I was one of the lucky ones who had only one profession, the one that everyone else envied. I only hope that what I've written about that exciting era has given you some sense of what it was like to walk into Paramount's Astoria Studio and bump into Rudolph Valentino or some other great and think nothing of it. They were all a part of what had become, during my youth, one of the foremost ingredients of the kaleidoscopic American scene. I'm grateful that I had the good fortune to have been there. It was an experience.

Then it happened. They started talking.

The picture industry was in a slump. The box office seemed to be suffering from a sudden, spreading sickness. Then the Warner Brothers came to the rescue with the talkies. The innovation brought back the dwindling patrons and drastically changed the whole movie set-up. *The New Yorker* ran a Peter Arno drawing of a Hollywood actor approaching a possible touch with, "C-c-could you lend me ten b-b-bucks until this talking thing b-b-blows over?" Poor man. It didn't blow. It took the country by storm.

Once more, I was among the lucky ones. Paramount had remade the first half of *The Canary Murder Case* as a talkie. Mal St. Clair had directed it. When the front office decided to redo the second half, St. Clair wasn't available. I got the job.

Naturally I was delighted to be given a crack at the new technique, but I inherited some problems. *The Canary Murder Case* was based on a book by S.S. Van Dine (Willard Huntington Wright). Philo Vance, the suave New York amateur detective, was played by William Powell, an experienced Broadway actor. Perfect. But the murdered showgirl, the Canary, had been played by Louise Brooks, and she was in Europe. We conducted a frantic search for an actress who could double Louise physically and could read lines. We finally persuaded Margaret Livingston, the wife of Paul Whiteman, to accept this thankless anonymous chore, and she did a great job. It was quite a trick. In the longer shots we were able to synchronize Miss Livingston's voice with Louise's lip movements, but

Lobby card for *The Canary Murder Case*, 1929.

there were portions of the second half of the picture where this wouldn't work. We finally devised a series of new scenes where the Canary could be photographed behind transparent curtains and partially hidden by a screen. All this took a lot of patience and ingenuity, but when *The Canary Murder Case* was released as a total talkie, the illusion that Louise Brooks was talking was never questioned—not even by the critics.

While we were editing *Canary*, Paramount bought *The Studio Murder Mystery*, which had been running as a serial in one of the fan magazines. The story concerned the killing of a Hollywood actor by a temperamental foreign director, who drove the corpse through the studio gate and ventriloquized his victim's voice so that the gateman could testify that the actor was alive when he left the studio that night. I agreed that this could be an effective gimmick, but the writing and the characterizations were pretty hackneyed.

When I was assigned the job of directing the yarn, I saw a chance to establish myself as a double-threat talking picture hep cat. Working day and night, I sketched out a series of scenes with dialogue and submitted the twenty-odd pages to producer Hector Turnbull. He thought they were promising, made some excellent suggestions, and okayed my writing the screenplay. With a salaam to my mentor, Austin Strong, I went to work with tremendous enthusiasm. Meanwhile, Hector Turnbull and the casting director assembled a notable array of performers.

Warner Oland, the original Charlie Chan, played the foreign director. This sterling "oriental" character actor was actually of Norwegian extraction. He gave his usual suave performance. For some strange reason he often blew his lines in the first take and swore angrily at himself. Having got rid of whatever mental quirk was responsible for his lapse, he was perfect. Eugene Pallette, who played Sergeant Heath in *Canary*, did another detective for us and we became fast friends. He loved comedy and good food, and was just beginning to put on the extra pounds which, together with his stentorian voice, were his trademarks in the many roles he played so well. Few of his fans remembered that he was Aramis in *The Three Musketeers* with Douglas Fairbanks. In our show, he was continually being ribbed by our amateur detective, the studio press agent, played by Neil Hamilton.

Neil had worked for me before opposite Esther Ralston. D.W. Griffith had discovered him when he was a photographic model for Arrow Collar ads. His performance in Griffith's *America* had won him immediate recognition. The industry's switch to talking pictures did cut short the careers of a few silent picture luminaries, but Neil who had never played a speaking part, took to the innovation as though he'd been in the theatre all his life. He had a particular gift for reading comedy speeches. His delivery of one line in *The Studio Murder Mystery* got a terrific laugh. Neil's hobby was magic. Like Chester Morris, Orson Welles, and director Cyril Endfield, Neil had a million of 'em up his sleeve.

A newcomer from the theatre had just been signed by Paramount and was given the part of the Hollywood star murdered by the director. His wife played opposite him. They were great troupers and wonderful people. A friendship I'm particularly proud of, developed between Fredric March, Florence Eldridge, and me.

The assistant director's job is one of the toughest in the business of making a film. His position might be likened to that of a top sergeant. He is the director's right-hand and his work is endless. He handles anything and everything that will simplify the complicated, distracting detail, which hovers like a swarm of flies over what goes on behind the camera. Between shots he picks the right moment to talk to the director about bit actors, costume tests, stock shots that have to be looked at after the rushes, sets that are being built, revisions in the shooting schedule, and so on, ad nauseam. In addition to all this, if he is particularly gifted, he will rough out the movement of crowds. When he has blocked out the scene and shown it to the director, they correct it together and it's ready to be shot.

My assistant on *The Studio Murder Mystery* was one of the ablest in the business. Shortly after the picture was completed, Henry Hathaway was assigned to direct *The Lives of a Bengal Lancer*, and since then he has become one of the top men in our field.

CHAPTER II

Studios have a tendency to typecast directors as well as actors so I was not surprised when my next assignment was *The Greene Murder Case*.

As a matter of fact, I was delighted because this was by all odds the best of the S.S. Van Dine mysteries. It had been adapted for the screen by Bartlett Cormack, whose play, *The Racket*, had brought Edward G. Robinson and John Cromwell to the Los Angeles theatre. The Warner Brothers immediately signed Robinson, and Paramount put Cromwell under contract as both an actor and a director. He had directed *The Racket* and played one of its leading roles.

Bart Cormack's screenplay was excellent. The story concerned the Greene family, which lived in a Charles Addams kind of house, overlooking the East River. With one exception, the Greenes were as disagreeable a collection of misanthropes as had ever been assembled between the covers of a book. The exception was the Cinderella of the family, a scorned half-sister. This part was beautifully played by a comparative newcomer, Jean Arthur. The rest of the cast, headed by William Powell as Vance and with Gene Pallette as Sergeant Heath, was everything a director could wish for.

Following the shooting of an obese brother and the wounding of Jean Arthur, Sergeant Heath and Philo Vance pay a visit to the weird house. After interviewing the unpleasant older sister (Florence Eldridge), they encounter the younger brother (Morgan Farley). This young man tells the visitors to mind their own business with bitter invective and walks out on them, slamming the door behind him. When the scene was over, Bill Powell, Gene Pallette, and I, held a conference. We all felt that this tirade called for a remark from Heath that would relieve the tension with a laugh. But what? After a half dozen fumbles, Gene came up with a

Newspaper advertisement for *Sweetie*, 1929.

straight line that we thought might do the trick. Gene looked solemnly at his erudite companion and said, "Mr. Vance, do you like this family?" I can only tell you that at the preview, the laugh lasted through the fadeout and into the following sequence.

Vance's sleuthing finally unearths the killer. In the Greene library he finds a German handbook of crime with detailed descriptions of murders that baffled the police for months. When he stumbles on a case where a suicide, anxious to give his death the appearance of a murder, had stood on a bridge and shot himself with a gun to which he had attached a weight so that it would plunge into the river, Vance remembered that heavy banks of snow were piled up around the Greene house when the fat brother was killed and Jean Arthur was wounded. Sergeant Heath sees what Vance is driving at. Jean Arthur could have shot herself and the weighted gun could have been pulled out the open window into a snowdrift. As they are discussing this, Vance learns that Jean Arthur is on the roof with her half-sister, Florence Eldridge. Vance climbs out a window and calls out a warning just as Jean Arthur rushes at Florence to shove her off the roof. Florence twists aside and the murderess plunges to her death in the icy river below.

I'm sure you can see what a brilliantly unexpected piece of casting it was to have an actress like Jean Arthur play the demented killer.

As it turned out, my fear that I'd be typed as a murder mystery director was groundless. My next assignment was a musical, *Sweetie*, written by George Marion, Jr. in a collaboration with Lloyd Corrigan. Shortly after this, Lloyd abandoned his writing career and switched to acting. His immediate success in this new field has continued until today.

George Marion's original title for the musical had been *Sis Boom Barbara!*, but the sales department had felt that it needed a label with more drawing power. Their reasoning is still a greater mystery to me than any of those that Philo Vance solved. The yarn, based on *The Charm School*, concerned a musical comedy star played by Nancy Carroll, who inherits a boy's prep school. The romance involved Nancy and Stanley Smith, who played the school's football captain. He writes her a song (courtesy of George Marion and Richard Whiting). I still remember the opening lines of the chorus.

> I composed a love song,
> Really rather neat,
> Calling the above song,
> "My Sweeter than Sweet."
> And, if I should ever lose you,
> All my dreams are wrecked.
> You mean the world to me—
> Or words to that effect.

All of George's lyrics were on the sophisticated side. He wrote one for Jack Oakie, who played a hoofer who had come to the school with Nancy, which gave Jack a chance to do a brilliant imitation of Al Jolson.

Oakie felt that the school song, "Alma Mater," was too solemn and dolorous. It should be jazzed up. Kneeling, sobbing, and smiting his chest, he delivered his version with a syncopated, "Alma Mammy!"

The cast included Stuart Erwin and the "boop-oop-a-doop" girl, Helen Kane. Stu played left guard on the football team. His scholastic standing fell considerably short of the minimum requirements, so his fellow students tutored him to ensure his passing a crucial test before the big game. George Marion wrote the following reply for Stu when a classmate asked him to define a preposition. "A preposition," Stu said, "is when you ask a girl will she."

Nancy Carroll was a triple-threat performer. She was an accomplished singer and dancer as well as a versatile actress. In private life she would stick sly pins into your ego with her Irish wit. I remember passing her on the back lot on my way to play tennis. White flannels were *de rigueur* in those days and I was wearing a white sweater. I thought I looked pretty sharp. Nancy's costume was one of Edith Head's delightful creations. I complimented Nancy. "You look very well yourself," she said, "for a bottle of milk!"

When Gary Cooper died the whole world seemed to stop whatever it was doing and took its hat off. To those of us who had worked with him the blow was more personal of course, and yet the image of Gary as a strong, silent man was quite correct. Despite his friendly warmth, he never let you get really close.

The picture we did together was *Only the Brave*. During the shooting, when the hipless Gary strode around the set's environs in what seemed to be a brown study, feminine visitors used to ask me what he was thinking about. Usually I shook my head and shrugged, but if their question came when I was struggling with some tough problem, and the interruption annoyed me, I sometimes told them the truth. "He's probably looking for a set with a bed in it," I said, "so he can lie down and take a nap." Gary was friendly and loaded with charm, but he was temperamentally somewhat aloof, just as Ronald Colman was. I am sure this detachment added to his appeal. Where the ladies are concerned, a retreating male back seems to create an almost irresistible challenge.

Only the Brave was an original comedy by one of my closest friends, Keene Thompson. The dialogue was by Edward Paramore, who had attended the Hill School when I was there and who was famous for his parodies of Robert W. Service, notably, *The Hermit of Shark Tooth Shoal*.

L. Keene Thompson's story was an amusing twist of the ancient Civil War cliché about the Southern girl falling in love with the Union spy, as in William Gillette's play, *Secret Service*. In Keene's yarn, the spy *wanted* the Southern Belle (played by Mary Brian) to catch him, because the dispatches he was carrying were designed to misinform the rebels. The picture opened with General Grant explaining the importance of the mission to Gary.

Phillips Holmes, the son of Taylor Homes, played Mary's beau. A fine young actor, Phil gave an excellent performance. In my opinion, Mary Brian was one of the most underrated actresses in pictures. A child star, she had first attracted attention as Wendy in *Peter Pan*. When she grew up, she was cast in countless ingénue roles. As a result of this ingénue tag, her fellow workers treated her as though she were their kid sister. The most hardboiled grips smothered their cuss words when she was around. I soon discovered that she was an imp and full of merry hell. But the sweet scent of a hothouse flower clung to her. It was not until her fine emotional acting opposite Gary Cooper in *The Virginian* that the public had a chance to see what a fine actress she really was, and even after that moving performance, they continued to cast her as an ingénue. In *Only the Brave*, she was an entrancing comedienne and had some fine serious moments to boot-and believe me, she didn't boot them. A wonderful actress and a wonderful gal!

My Scotch grandfather should have been with me one bra' day during the shooting of *Only the Brave*. Sir Harry Lauder visited our set and was photographed with the cast and the director. From beginning to end, directing *Only the Brave* was a joy.

The Benson Murder Case was the least interesting of the series dealing with the detective work of Philo Vance. Aside from the pleasure of working once more with Bill Powell and Gene Pallette, I recall almost nothing about the picture except that William Boyd—not the noted movie actor but the Sergeant Quirt of the stage production of *What Price Glory?*—was in our cast and so was Katherine DeMille, the adopted daughter of Cecil B. Her part in *The Benson Murder Case* was one of her first. Before long, she was playing top roles, which she won the right to play with no help at all from the great C.B.

My next job was directing Clara Bow's first talkie, *True to the Navy*. Her leading man was Fredric March, who gave a superlative performance as a tough gunner's mate. Clara's role was that of a waitress in a café fre-

Lobby card for *True to the Navy*, 1930.

quented by sailors when their battle wagons were in port. One of the sailors was played by Rex Bell, who married Clara shortly after the picture was finished. Rex is now the Attorney General of Nevada, with a keen interest in boy's clubs and many other worthwhile extracurricular activities.

One fine day Clara's navy beaux all arrive simultaneously at the café. In the battle royal which ensues, the rival gobs demolish the joint. The proprietor of the place arrives just in time to find Clara alone and miserable in the midst of the wreckage. He smites his forehead and mutters as only Harry Green could mutter, "I wonder if I'm covered."

Clara gave a fine account of herself and Freddy March did a great job in his—for him—offbeat role. The reason I shan't go into the ups and downs of Keene Thompson's story is that my recollection of them has been snowed under by the memory of an accident which shocked us all when we were about two-thirds through our shooting.

Clara was playing an angry scene with Freddy which climaxed with her knocking a stack of crockery off a countertop. I had carefully arranged the things so that everything within Clara's reach had been rounded off or else was the conventional material made of candy glass called "breakaway."

Two real glass goblets were far out of her reach—I thought. Knowing Clara as well as I did, I should have had them removed. She played the scene magnificently, but worked herself up to such a high pitch of fury that her final wild swing knocked over the glasses and on the back sweep opened up a gash in her hand from the base of her little finger to her wrist. When the blood spurted out Clara screamed. Freddy grabbed her hand and pressed it tightly above the cut, which stopped the bleeding until the doctor got there.

The next day a still shaky Clara appeared with a tight, skin-colored bandage. For the rest of the week she had to favor the hand. I don't believe I have ever felt so guilty. Why hadn't I junked those goblets? I had nightmares about it. Clara was all forgiving, but—I'm sure you'll understand why my subconscious has buried the plot detail of *True to the Navy*.

The coffee break which follows will deal with photography, sound, and special effects in the early thirties. If you're fearful this may be a dull interlude, by all means skip it, but if you're at all interested in the technical aspects of picture making, you can count on one phase of the discussion which may make it practically painless. I am a mechanical moron. I have only the vaguest idea what goes on under the hood of my car; so if I can understand what I'm talking about in this brief digression, you should have no trouble at all.

Even non-mechanically-minded viewers will agree, I believe, that the quality of motion picture photography improved noticeably in the time span between *The Great Train Robbery* and *True to the Navy*. For one thing the film itself was developed enormously in the matter of its sensitivity and it will continue to be improved in this respect. The same improvement took place in such items as lenses, filters, and color. But this is only part of the story. The cameramen themselves inspired the creation of new techniques. New lighting and new lights were discovered. The cameramen studied the compositions of great painters which advanced their own arrangements of people and objects. To this skill they added the ability to compose for shots in which the actors and the camera moved. In this field a fascinating and helpful apparatus is the boom. This contraption has a long steel arm. On one end of this arm the cameramen and the director are seated, and on the other, a counterbalance of adjustable weights can be arranged in perfect equilibrium so that a specially trained technician can swing the camera and its operators to an exact position with almost no effort. The whole apparatus is on a truck which the grips can move back and forward on a track. Thus a scene can start with a higher long shot and end up with the close-up of an actor or vice versa.

The placing of the camera is usually the result of a conference between the director and the head cameraman. If they have worked together a lot, the decision is usually arrived at in a few minutes. In the case of a veteran like John Seitz, my favorite cameraman, there is almost no discussion. John, who shot *The Four Horsemen of the Apocalypse* for Rex Ingram when they were both youngsters, sets up the camera quickly and asks me to have a peek. With John I usually don't look through the finder until the shot is fully rehearsed and we're all ready to go.

An interesting photographic development which was perfected in the early thirties is the process shot. Perhaps the best way to describe a process shot is to talk about an example of the trick. Imagine two people seated opposite one another in a train traveling through the French countryside, which can be seen through the window. Behind the actors is a translucent screen and some distance beyond the screen is a projection booth. From this booth a moving picture of the French scenery is thrown upon the scene. This movie was taken in France from the window of a real train, using a special super-steady camera. In the Hollywood studio the regular camera—synchronized with the projector—simultaneously photographs the actors in the foreground and the projected countryside beyond them. When the background shots were made in France, they also included three quarter angles shooting forward and backward, so that close angle shots of the actors can be made in the studio. From this explanation you now understand, I hope, how performers can appear against all sorts of exotic backgrounds without ever leaving Hollywood.

In the early days of the talkies, the old-fashioned bulky cameras were hidden in booths at various angles—close and far away—and the cameras all photographed the scene simultaneously. By using telescopic lenses, some of the cameras took head close-ups. This meant that the whole area had to be lighted and the quality of the close-ups suffered. Then, too, the microphones had to be hung out of range of the long shot cameras or concealed behind flower vases and other props to get the intimate sound quality for the close-ups. During this early period the mikes didn't move. When the actors walked as they were talking, the soundman turned the microphones off and on as the player passed them.

Before long, the technicians built new cameras which were soundless and much more compact. They also added the sound boom to the talking picture equipment. This boom is a collapsible pole with a mike suspended from it which follows the actors as they move. Today the mike

A Christmas card cartoon drawn by Frank Tuttle.

is constructed so that its sensitive side can be twisted toward the actor who is talking and back to the second actor when he replies. The technique of sound recording has made giant strides. Originally the volume of sound that could be recorded was limited in its range, but today it is possible to record an explosion which would shatter the windows in a theatre if it were played back at its full volume.

Special effects are the Hollywood name for trick shots. A well-known example is the split screen. By photographing one side of the screen at a time an actor can play a scene with himself—as a twin brother for instance. Another special effects trick is the use of glass shots. Instead of building a huge set, only the lower section where the action takes place is constructed. The upper section is painted black on a large plate glass close to the camera. Later an artist wipes away the black and paints a meticulous reproduction of the upper stories of the building to match the constructed lower section. Obviously this can be done at a fraction of the cost of building the total structure.

Miniature shots are another item in the special effects bag of tricks. Ships, airplanes, and trains are wrecked, set on fire, and blown up in miniature. Nowadays the technicians who build and photograph all these "now you see it, now you don't" elements in the making of motion pictures are so expert that it is impossible to detect where the reality stops and their magic begins.

CHAPTER 12

Following *True to the Navy*, I did two more talkies with Clara, *Her Wedding Night* and *No Limit*. I've already mentioned that the first of these was a remake of *Miss Bluebeard* and told you about the compliment Charlie Ruggles paid Ray Griffith when he refused to change any of the business which Ray had created in the silent version. *No Limit* was the picture in which Clara had the temporary difficulty with the wedding service responses, but there were some other incidents connected with this one, which I believe are worth describing.

The company went to New York to shoot our exteriors. One of the players was in the dumps because she would be separated from a young singer she was engaged to. His name was Harry L. Crosby—the great Bing. Dixie Lee was a first-rate actress and a delightful person. She married Bing shortly after we returned from New York.

One of the most difficult scenes to record and photograph was shot in front of a movie theatre on Sixty-Sixth Street, with the elevated trains rattling by in the background and street traffic whirling by in both directions. The action involved Clara, Dixie, and Stu Erwin walking along and talking while the camera trucked back in front of them. The police were a great help, but you can imagine how difficult the problem was when you consider that hundreds of people never stopped watching from early afternoon until late the same night. Before every take I begged the onlookers to be as quiet as possible and asked the police to clear the entire area behind the actors so that our extras could fill this space in order to be sure that no one would wander into the scene and stare at the camera.

Jack Goodrich, our soundman, was enormously skillful and patient, but it took twenty-seven takes to get one that he would okay. When we saw it in the rushes, we agreed it was worth the trouble. You could understand every word and the noise of the L trains and the taxi horns was audible in the background but subdued to a point where it was not too obtrusive, thanks to Jack Goodrich's clever manipulation of his recording dials.

During the night shooting, a tall man in a dinner jacket strolled up to me and asked if he could talk to Clara, who was having coffee inside the movie theatre. He said that he knew her but he'd been busy at Madison Square Garden knocking someone out. Then I recognized him—Slapsie Maxie Rosenbloom. I took him into the theatre. Clara said hello and they passed the time of night. As you can see, my profession is crazy, but it's seldom dull.

Contrariwise, *Dude Ranch* skidded pretty close to be a dull assignment except for its fine cast and one stuntman. Jack Oakie, Gene Pallette, and Stu Erwin were our comedians and the leading lady was the lovely June Collier who met Stu during the shooing of *Dude Ranch* and married him shortly afterwards.

The stunt man, Billy Jones, was the younger brother of one of the writers of our script, Grover Jones. The stunt Billy did for us in *Dude Ranch* was really spectacular. In the open rear end of a carnival wagon which has skidded to a stop in the path of an oncoming express train, Jack Oakie, in a cowboy outfit, is fighting with one of the heavies. Just before the locomotive smashes the wagon to smithereens his opponent lands a right cross on Jack's chin knocking him out of the wagon—to safety.

Obviously a stunt like this can only be photographed once so it is shot from several angles and its preparation takes a long time. Everything metal had been removed from the wagon, and its catty-cornered position across the tracks was arranged to give all the cameras a good view of the stunt. Mattresses, covered with dirt, were placed for Billy to land on under his direction. Then our train backed up for its start. While all this was going on, a half dozen stuntmen, friends of Billy Jones, showed up. They discussed the stunt with Billy. Just before we were ready to go, I cautioned Billy not to wait too long before making his dive. I pointed out that the cameramen would under-crank, which would increase the speed of the train and make the miss seem closer than it would really be. Billy looked over the situation once more and said he was ready whenever we were.

The stuntmen took a position outside of camera range but where they could get a good view of the inside of the wagon and where Billy would be hidden from the cameras until just before the train crashed into the wagon. The train would be doing about thirty-five when it hit. We signaled the engineer to start.

Billy was wearing black sneakers instead of shoes to give himself a surer takeoff. When the train was about thirty-five feet away, he decided to give his watching friends an extra thrill. Out of the camera range, he bent over and tied his right shoelace. Then he dived. I have a still picture of the locomotive smashing into the wagon. *Billy's body is still in the air!*

A few weeks after this, I gave a party at my house for about fifteen of my stunt men pals. I shall never forget what went on at this little gathering of the faithful. I remember watching one of them conversing casually with his closest friend in a loveseat near the fireplace. To emphasize a point he picked up a poker and tapped his buddy on the shin. Pal Joey told him to quit. He kept right on tapping. The tappee extended his hand and shoved the lighted end of his cigarette into the poker-wielding fist. The tapping stopped.

One of the stunt men was their patsy. He would risk his neck for a hundred bucks but he was not exactly the intellectual type. His playmates slipped a fistful of my best silver into his pocket. Later someone asked him for a cigarette. He reached into his pocket and came up with two spoons and a butter knife. They shook reproving fingers at him. How could he be such a miserable thief—and in the home of their amigo? He blushed and stammered. I just couldn't play straight, but even when I told him he'd been framed, he kept on apologizing. It took several minutes to snap him out of it.

To break up the embarrassing moment, I urged everyone to wander out to the swimming pool and the lawn. What ensued was a series of nip-ups, pratfalls, collapsing human pyramids, and hundred and eights—stuntman slang for a somersault through the air. By the time the party was over, my sides ached from laughing.

One of my guests was Jack Holbrook, the pivotal figure in a true story about stunt men. Several months before my party, Jack was chosen with four of his pals to do a fight sequence on a bridge. The director who did the picking was unaware that Jack had been temporarily blinded in a movie slugfest a few weeks before. Jack needed the money to make a big payment on a loan. His pals had stood close to him during the interview so that his blindness would not be noticed.

When they did the fight on the bridge, the other stuntmen guided him with whispered directions. He threw punches, took them, and finally fell off the bridge into a net. Happy ending. He got a big check and paid off the loan.

Lobby card for *Love Among the Millionaires*, 1930.

There is practically nothing these wonderful guys won't do, and they plan their routines with infinite care to minimize the chances of being seriously hurt. They work out the action so that it will photograph most effectively, and many of them are excellent actors. I am proud to be their friend.

I just took a quick gander of the list of pictures I've directed and discovered that one of them, *Love Among the Millionaires*, a musical starring Clara Bow, is chronologically in the wrong spot. I should have mentioned it much earlier. Sorry. Clara sang in it, and very well. Mitzi Green, one of the most remarkable child performers ever, did an imitation of Clara singing one of her numbers. Today Mitzi is grown up and married, but when she appeared in *Love Among the Millionaires* she was ten. There was a curious "twisteroo" to her impersonation of Clara. Paramount asked us to finish with Mitzi as soon as possible because she was scheduled to start in another picture. We hadn't yet photographed Clara's number, so I asked her if she'd do it for Mitzi. She was delighted to and gave it a fine rendition. Right after this we shot Mitzi's imitation and it was terrific. The only trouble was that when we photographed Clara singing a week or so later, her performance bore little resemblance to what she'd shown Mitzi. All speed and no control, Clara just naturally topped herself. When she saw Clara's performance Mitzi was heartbroken, but her takeoff had caught the essence of Clara. The difference in detail was unnoticed by the audiences who applauded Mitzi like crazy.

Another fine performer in *Millionaires* was Skeets Gallagher, whom I'd seen on Broadway when he starred in a musical version of the John Barrymore vehicle, *The Fortune Hunter*. In our picture Mitzi played a precocious youngster who kept getting in Skeets' hair. After one encounter he turned on her and remarked that if he were ever electrocuted he would love to hold her on his lap. Mitzi's reply in the script was, "Don't be common!" Just before we shot the scene Mitzi solemnly asked me if I thought it would be funnier if she said, "Don't be plebeian!" I told her I thought it would.

Mitzi's parents were vaudevillians who adored her, but I felt it was too bad that she had so few chances to get out and play like other children. I suggested to her mother and father that I'd love to take them all to the Los Angeles Tennis Club some Sunday and have Norval Craig, one of the club's pros, give Mitzi a tennis lesson. They thought it was a fine idea so I set it up for the following Sunday. It was fascinating to watch Mitzi's concentration when Norval showed her the first principles of developing a correct forehand and backhand. When the lesson was over, Norval took me aside and told me that if he could work with Mitzi for six months, he would make a champion out of her. But Mitzi's stiff picture schedule prevented her continuing with the lessons, and so "old lady Green," as Jack Oakie used to call Mitzi, was lost to the world of Wills and Mallory. Ah, well, we and the vast audience that loved her, still had this delightful young lady. Lucky us!

Skeets Gallagher read the famous line, "You know what a hen's doing when she flaps her wings and cackles after she lays and egg? She's *advertising!*" in the screen version of *It Pays to Advertise*, the Broadway hit play.

For me, the biggest kick in staging this Paramount picture was my introduction to its star, Carole Lombard. You may not remember this, and it may sound incredible, but the most formidable obstacle in Carole's progress to the top had been her beauty. They wouldn't let her act. They kept telling her just to be there. They assured her that all she had to do was walk on in a lovely gown and the audience would be very happy. But Carole wasn't. She kept begging for a chance to show what she could do. It was months before anyone would let her play a dramatic scene, and it took even longer before the powers that be discovered her unique talent for comedy, a talent which she later displayed with telling effect in such pictures as *My Man Godfrey*.

Fortunately for me, her role in *It Pays to Advertise* gave her a fine chance to exploit her rare gift. Among Carole's many winning qualities was her appreciation of the talents of her fellow players. Skeets Gallagher, Gene Pallette, and Norman Foster were all adept at getting the most out of funny lines and situations and their expert performances delighted Carole Lombard. Everyone on the set adored her. Like Aileen Pringle, she would occasionally cut loose with censorable comments but she usually saved them for some prudish listener she thought needed to be shocked. One department head at Paramount was such a person. Carole would corner him and ask him questions that had her straight-laced victim stammering and blushing and the rest of us swallowing the laughs her sallies provoked.

When we were about half way through our shooting schedule, we suddenly realized that if we stepped up our tempo we could finish *It Pays to Advertise* in time to be free for New Year's Eve. Boy, did we start moving! The crew put on the pressure too. They were as eager as the rest of us to be on the town for the holiday.

Late in the afternoon of our last day's work, we were handed a bombshell, an extra page of dialogue which the foreign department had told Ben Schulberg, the head of the studio, would add considerably to the sales value of our picture in the British Commonwealth. Unlike most movies, *It Pays to Advertise* mentioned a whole string of actual products by name, after having them cleared by Paramount's legal department. The new scene featured an additional list of articles, which included such British items as Craven A Cigarettes, Eno's Fruit Salts, etc., etc.

I have never seen actors memorize so many unfamiliar words so fast. At 6:45, we were ready to go. Gene Pallette had the last speech—a long one extolling the virtues of dozens of English products. Gene finished in a burst of glory, took a deep breath, looked straight into the camera and hollered, "Okay, Schulberg. That's the last word you'll get out of me *this year!*"

Later our spies told us that Ben had yelled with delight at Gene's unexpected ad lib.

CHAPTER 13

This Is the Night originated as an idea suggested to producer Barney Glazer by composer Ralph Rainger. Ralph's first popular song hit, "Moanin' Low," had been featured in Dwight Wiman's first *Little Show*. Ralph was exceptionally talented and, unlike many of the songwriters of that period, was as much interested in creating musical ideas as in writing hit songs, although he composed scores of them too. Ralph's idea was to open a picture in Paris with a series of rhythmic shots in which the action moved in time with the music. A waiter, for instance, would pile a stack of French plates with the price of the drink on them in tempo. This kind of action would segue into a scene showing Roland Young helping Thelma Todd out of a car and his driver slamming the door and catching Thelma's skirt which would rip off. The passersby would start chanting, "Madame has lost her dress! Madame has lost her dress. From Brest to Nice, let all work cease. Madame has lost her dress!" These lyrics were written by George Marion, who also wrote the dialogue for *This Is the Night*, Barney Glazer supplying the plot structure. Their yarn went on to disclose that Thelma's fiancé was an Olympic javelin thrower, played by a newcomer to the Hollywood scene, Cary Grant. This character was violently jealous, and when we met him he carried his javelins in a sort of golf bag gimmick on his back. His suspicion that Roland had been carrying on an affair with his girl forced Roland to acquire a wife—and quickly—to divert the javelin thrower's deadly jealousy. Roland hires a French movie star, played by Lili Damita, to pretend to be his wife.

Ralph Rainger's musical treatment was followed throughout the telling of our farcical yarn, which involved Charlie Ruggles as a friend of Roland, and wound up in a gondola chase through the canals of Venice—conveniently located as a wonderfully constructed set on the United Artists' back lot.

Obviously the success of this kind of musical nonsense depends largely on the skill of the players, the dialogue, and the musical background. Fortunately, in *This Is the Night*, those elements were all there. I'll give you one brief sample of the sort of thing George Marion contributed.

Cary Grant has cornered Lili Damita in the dining car on the boat train from Paris, and is checking on Roland's claim that she is his wife. Roland is seated at the next table with his back to the inquisitor. He has borrowed Lili's makeup mirror so that his reflection can whisper promptings which his "wife" can see. Cary asks her where she and Roland were living. Roland's lips form the word "Cincinnati!" Lili isn't quite sure what he has said. Roland repeats, "Cin-Cincinnati!" Lili smiles at Cary and says, "We were living in sin." Cary and Roland react. Roland shakes his head and enunciates his correction. "-natti-natti!" he says. Lili lowers her eyes and demurely declares, "We were naughty." Which doesn't help.

I had first met Roland Young in New York during the Film Guild days and it was a real joy to work with this accomplished comedian. Drunk scenes can be pretty corny, but George Marion wrote one for Roland and Charlie Ruggles, which was a classic and which, in their able hands, was a laugh bonanza. Lili Damita did a fine job with her role, aided, as always, by that fabulous face and figure. Contrary to what this superb equipment might lead one to expect, she was a hardworking and skilled performer and a delightful person.

Cary Grant hated his acting in *This Is the Night*, but if you've seen his Paramount debut on the TV late show recently, I'm sure you'll agree with me that he did a good job.

During the shooting of *This Is the Night* one of Barney Glazer's assistants was a young Romanian painter who gave me a number of excellent suggestions for unusual camera angles. Since then, he has become a top director, with a long list of successful pictures. His name is Jean Negulesco.

Shortly after this, someone at Paramount came up with an idea, which promised to be a sure-fire box office show to be called *The Big Broadcast*. It would feature the top names in radio, Kate Smith, Burns and Allen, Cab Calloway, Connie Boswell, The Street Singer, Vincent Lopez and his orchestra, and many more. Once again Barney Glazer cooked up a story with George Marion. This one would exploit the adventures of an irresponsible young radio star and a young lady who was worshipped by a shy admirer. These characters would be played by Leila Hyams and Stu Erwin. The young radio star would play himself—Bing Crosby.

At this time Bing was one of the top singers on the air, but his acting experience was limited to a series of shorts he had made under the Mack Sennett banner. Barney Glazer and I ran several of them. Aside from the Crosby voice and charm, they were pretty bad. Bing didn't seem to know what to do with his hands. His features were attractive, except for his ears which, like Clark Gable's, were not as close to his head as cameramen like them to be. We made some tests with them gummed back and his handsome puss looked fine.

When we started shooting, Bing was extremely cooperative and his sense of comedy was first-rate from the opening shot. I cautioned him about his tendency to over-gesticulate and we found ways to eliminate unnecessary hand movements. The camera makes what is happening seem more real than a stage performance where everything has to be projected. Bing's vocal style was ideal for moving pictures. His approach was casual and he liked to move around. We worked out interesting pieces of business so that he wouldn't have to just stand there and deliver a number.

I'd been a Crosby fan long before we began shooting *The Big Broadcast*. I considered him the most exciting popular singer we'd had in years, but he was much more than that. The experts in the music department assured me that he was one of the most naturally musical performers ever. Aside from the appealing quality of his baritone, his individual sense of broken rhythm was remarkable. As we progressed with the picture, Bing's acting improved enormously. And, as had been the case with many other players I've mentioned, he liked to work with top actors and learn from them. Between shots he spoke a language of his own, a slang-enriched "Americanese" that is almost impossible to describe, but was as amusing as it was unique.

Ralph Rainger's music for *Broadcast* included two hit tunes, "Here Lies Love" and "Please." Leo Robin wrote the lyrics. Later, he and Ralph joined forces and became a permanent Paramount team. George Marion's dialogue was up to the high standard he had already set for himself. Our picture marked the first time at bat in a major picture for Burns and Allen, whose material was written by George and his brother. Gracie and George had only recently perfected their offbeat approach in which George played straight for Gracie's insane logic. The result was a kind of "Gracie in Wonderland" fantasy which was literally out of this world.

Eventually our troupe journeyed to New York to photograph the specialties of Kate Smith, Cab Calloway, and the rest of the radio stars. My Film Guild colleague, Fred Waller, had charge of this interlude. Fred had arranged a well-planned schedule for us, and the radio personalities put on a great show. Barney Glazer had asked us to give him a choice of two numbers from each performer. All the radio stars were most cooperative, and we returned to Hollywood with everything Barney had asked for. *The Big Broadcast* hit the jackpot.

In the silent days the Rockett Brothers had made a notable contribution to the screen by producing a fine picture about Abraham Lincoln. Since then, Al Rockett had been signed as a producer at Fox. It was under his guidance that I directed Warner Baxter in *Dangerously Yours*. Warner's hobby was cooking, and during our picture I was privileged to sample one of his superb dinners. I can give him no higher praise than to tell you he was as fine a cook as he was an actor. He was also keenly interested in out-of-the-ordinary writing and gave me a fascinating book, *The History of Human Stupidity*, which I thoroughly enjoyed.

Al Rockett surrounded Warner Baxter with a distinguished cast which included Florence Eldridge and Mischa Auer. Mischa, grandson of the great violin teacher, Leopold Auer, had broken into pictures by showing an agent a series of character studies of himself in a variety of make-ups. He was a terrific clown. Shortly after playing a Hindu mystic for me in *Dangerously Yours*, he was entertaining some friends of mine and did an uproarious impersonation of a gorilla. Among my guests was Gregory La Cava. Mischa's clowning paid off. Gregory introduced Mischa's gorilla to moviegoers in *My Man Godfrey*.

Cameraman John Seitz photographed the Warner Baxter picture. We took an instant liking to one another. John used to tear his hair when something displeased him and shout, "No, no, NO!" Actually Johnny is one of the gentlest men I have ever known, and I suspected that the hair pulling was an act to shock people. I think he feared they might not be impressed by his normally gentle manners.

Like most comedy melodramas, *Dangerously Yours* was not at all spectacular, but I thoroughly enjoyed directing it, and it did very well at the box office.

Dangerously Yours was B.Z.—before Zanuck—at Fox, but Winfield Sheehan, the head of the studio at that time, apparently liked my direction because he borrowed me again from Paramount to stage *Pleasure Cruise*, with Roland Young and Genevieve Tobin.

Our screenplay was the work of Guy Bolton, famous on Broadway as the book writer for the successful team of Wodehouse, Bolton, and Kern. It was the best comedy screenplay I'd ever been asked to direct.

Directors usually have a number of suggestions for changes, particularly if they've been writers themselves, but I shot *Pleasure Cruise* exactly as it was written with one tiny exception.

The plot was a variation of Molnar's *The Guardsman*. In Guy Bolton's story, Genevieve Tobin has a responsible job, but her husband, Roland Young, is temporarily out of work and is forced to hold up his end by washing the dishes and making himself generally useful around the house. As if this weren't bad enough, he is haunted by visions of attractive young men at the office flirting with his pretty wife. The situation takes a turn for the worse when she decides to go on a pleasure cruise for her fortnight's holiday. Roland rebels. Unknown to his wife, he gets himself a job as the barber on the *S.S. Whatever*, and goes along so that he can keep an eye on his darling.

Just as he had feared, a handsome bachelor, played by Ralph Forbes, shows up and makes an immediate play for the lovely Genevieve. Comes the night of the gala when everyone is in costume and wine is flowing like wine, and Forbes pleads with Genevieve to leave her cabin door unlocked. Roland gets wind of this and ties and gags the would-be philanderer, leaving him struggling in his cabin.

It was the preparation for the next key scene that I took a few liberties with. I had always felt that the wife in *The Guardsman*—and I felt the same way about this scene—would recognize her husband even in the dark, so I gave the build-up an added fill up to take care of this implausibility. I showed Genevieve Tobin in bed, drinking rather lavishly as she toyed with temptation. She peered at Roland's picture on her dressing table. With the help of the special effects department, his image frowned and shook its head. Genevieve gave him a reassuring smile, slipped out of bed, stumbled tipsily to the door and locked it, but the door was slightly ajar and she didn't actually lock it. With a virtuous bow to Roland's picture, she weaved back to bed and put out the lights—so we didn't even have to fade out.

Guy Bolton's funniest scene took place the next morning when Ralph came to apologize for not having shown up. His conversation with Genevieve was loaded with double entendre. She thinks that Ralph is apologizing for his last night's performance and assures him that on the contrary!

The truth finally comes out when Roland shows up, and all's well that ends well in the house of Young.

CHAPTER 14

I'm sure it was Eddie Cantor who got me my next job directing the Samuel Goldwyn production of *Roman Scandals* in which Eddie would star. Our relationship had been so cordial during the filming of *Kid Boots* that I felt certain he had asked the great Goldwyn to see if I were available.

The preliminary deal worked out by my agent was that Goldwyn would pay for my trip to and from New York to attend a reading of the treatment written by George Kaufman and Robert Sherwood. The reading took place in Goldwyn's hotel suite. Naturally I was all steamed up at the prospect of hearing a story outline by two of the finest playwrights in America. Eddie and Arthur Hornblow, Jr., Goldwyn's right-hand man, were also present when Kaufman read the treatment.

After the authors had left, Goldwyn asked us all for our reactions. When it came to my turn, I said that the general idea was fresh, original, and full of wonderful possibilities. However I did feel that the screenplay would need a lot more hard work, and that the climax to the Roman episode, in which the Vandals descended upon Rome, was a weak finish for a Cantor musical. Mr. G bridled. I would have to agree, he said, that seventy-five percent of what we had heard was sensational. I replied that it wasn't a question of percentages. The concept was certainly all that anyone could ask for, but the detail would need a great deal of sharpening and broadening. Like all comedians, Eddie had to have assorted gags and funny lines. The treatment offered fine opportunities for this kind of material, but it still had to be written. Above all, I repeated, the yarn must have a whirlwind finish and a funny one. Eddie's last picture, *The Kid from Spain*, directed by Leo McCarey, one of the all-time greats in the field of comedy, ended with a bullfight which had topped everything else in the show. To follow such a winner with something less spectacular would, in my opinion, be a fatal mistake. Eddie backed me up in this and I quickly added that it must be obvious that there were only three climax possibilities for a story dealing with ancient Rome. Eddie must either fight gladiators, be thrown to the lions, or become involved in a chariot race, which would be my choice. Goldwyn screamed that he wouldn't spend all that money. I said quickly that once you had a picture called *Roman Scandals* you were stuck with a big finish. I begged for permission to come back the next afternoon with a further development of some ideas that were simmering in the back of my head. Eddie and Arthur Hornblow added their pleas to mine. Goldwyn glowered but he agreed. In the corridor I told Eddie and Arthur what I had in mind and they liked it. We shook hands and parted.

The following afternoon I went into my act. First, I pointed out that the chariot race could be a cross-country chase so that no coliseum would have to be built. As I visualized it, Eddie would be carrying some sort of important message and the heavies would be trying to overtake and intercept him. When he first stepped into the chariot, his horses would take off so quickly that Eddie would be thrown out. His fellow conspirators would then nail Eddie's scandals to the floor of the chariot.

The chase would involve a series of obstacles and gags still to be devised; but the climax I had in mind would be the gradual disintegration of the chariot until Eddie found himself being dragged along on two splintered segments of the chariot's floor which would look like skis. The enthusiasm of Eddie Cantor and Arthur Hornblow for what I was describing finally won the argument. Mr. Goldwyn bought the idea. The meeting broke up and in a day or so I returned to Hollywood.

Shortly after this, William Anthony McGuire, a veteran writer for Flo Ziegfeld, was assigned to go to work on the screenplay, and later Arthur Sheikman and Nat Perrin, two top comedy writers, were added to the writing staff.

Without a doubt, Sam Goldwyn is a great showman. Perhaps his outstanding virtue is his instinctive feeling for what will make a picture great, plus his bulldog determination to give it every necessary embellishment. Besides these qualities he has surrounded himself over the years with a staff of departmental heads who are exceptionally able and wonderful to work with. Among his other characteristics Goldwyn has a great respect for writers, particularly established novelists and playwrights. He seems to be awestruck by their ability to snatch ideas from nowhere and set them down on paper by some kind of, to him, incomprehensible magic. There are a number of stories floating around that bear on his attitude toward the writing profession. The one I've selected to tell you may not even be true, but perhaps you'll find it amusing.

Goldwyn had bought a property which he wanted a well-known playwright to adapt into a screenplay. When the playwright had read the original and found out what Goldwyn had paid for the book, he hurried to urge him to put the property on the shelf and forget it. In his opinion no one would be able to convert it into a successful screenplay. Goldwyn quickly assured him that he would double his usual fee. "It's not a question of money, Sam," the writer said, "I wouldn't touch it if you paid me triple what you're offering. It's no good." The bulldog wouldn't take "no" for an answer. He pleaded, cajoled, and bullied, but the writer stuck to his guns and made one final plea for Goldwyn to junk the picture. But the great man was deaf to this questioning of his judgment. He made the film. It was a turkey—a rare phenomenon in "Goldwynland." Many months later the writer's agent brought up his name for a new project. Goldwyn stiffened. "Don't mention that man's name in this office," he said. "He is connected with one of my biggest flops!" True or false, I think the psychology laid bare by this remark is as unique as it is revealing.

Shortly after my return to Hollywood, I signed a standard contract at so much a week for ten weeks. If the shooting took longer than this I would be paid pro rata until the picture was finished, and the contract named a starting date. During the long interim before we started shooting, I frequently dropped into the studio to work out a motivation for the chariot chase and to elaborate the details of obstacles and gags. Constructing a comedy screenplay is a prodigious task. Some Hollywood sage once said that there can be all kinds of reactions to a dramatic story, but in the case of broad comedy, there can be only two. Either they laugh or they don't. I once mentioned to Arthur Hornblow that the writing seemed to be dragging on and on. He shrugged and said that had always been true with the Cantor spectaculars.

Meanwhile, preparations in all the other departments were rolling along. Busby Berkeley was assigned to stage the dancing. His particular talent was his use of the camera to photograph dances from novel and exciting angles. Before long he began to rehearse the choreography.

Another preliminary job was to test dozens of girls from whose number the chosen few would be glorified as "Goldwyn Girls." Experience had evolved a timesaving routine for this. Walter Mayo, one of the ablest assistants in Hollywood, explained it to me. Two cameras were set up several feet apart on one of the soundstages. The candidates appeared in bathing suits and Walter photographed them walking back and forth in a long shot. Following this each girl sat in a tall chair which could be revolved. Under my direction the chair was slowly twisted from one profile to the other, with a long pause for a straight-on shot in which the girl gave the camera her most winning smile. Incidentally, one of the fair ladies selected for *Roman Scandals* was Lucille Ball. Historians should note that this superb comedienne got her start as a Goldwyn Girl.

I had already decided that Ralph Ceder was the ideal second unit director to stage our chariot race. Ralph had directed for Mack Sennett and we had met when Ray Griffith had suggested him to direct a chase in *Time To Love*. Ralph was a stocky, handsome man with steel blue eyes. Everyone agreed that he was the man for the job and he began to round up Billy Jones, Chick Collins, and the rest of our stunt man buddies. All of them had a great respect for Ralph, who was tough to work for but would never ask anyone to do a stunt that he wouldn't do himself.

From Warner Brothers, Goldwyn borrowed Warren and Dubin to write the songs for *Roman Scandals*. Freddy Kohlmar, who has since produced innumerable successful pictures at Paramount and Columbia, was the Goldwyn casting director, and he engaged a fine group of actors for the show. Among them were Edward Arnold as the Roman emperor, Veree Teasdale, Adolphe Menjou's wife, as the empress, Alan Mowbray as the emperor's aide-de-camp, and Willard Robertson as the crooked political boss in the modern episode. The love story was beautified by Gloria Stuart, who played a British princess captured by the Romans. Opposite her was David Manners, exceptional among American actors in that he preferred costume roles to those in modern dress. During the shooting, by the way, Gloria Stuart met Arthur Sheikman, the writer I've already mentioned, and they were married shortly after the picture was completed.

All this preliminary backing and filling went on for months. Just before we were ready to go, my agent dropped into my office with a bombshell. Goldwyn had sent for him and given us an ultimatum. I had now been on the payroll for my ten weeks minimum guarantee. The great man had declared that what I had already received was all he could afford to pay me. Either I would direct the picture without further remuneration or he would get someone else. The first alternative was an obvious violation of my contract, but it was just as obvious that he had me over the well-known barrel. *Roman Scandals* would be a Goldwyn epic. My name on the screen as its director would be a great talking point for my agent when he negotiated future deals. It was futile to argue that Goldwyn could have told us this months earlier and given us the chance to make another picture elsewhere before he was ready to start. He hadn't and that was that.

To beat your breast when you've been outsmarted in a business deal is practically un-American. In the history of money making in this country, sharp practice is traditionally admired. Read it and weep. Many of America's vast fortunes were founded by deft dealers of one kind or another. If the deck has been stacked, don't holler. It was take it or leave it. We took it. The picture started.

One morning a week or so later, during the shooting of the modern episode, an enraged figure brushed me aside and confronted a prominent player. "You're the heavy!" the intruder shouted. "Stop trying to get laughs!" The accuser did an about face and strode off the set. It was Goldwyn. The actor, a distinguished character man who was also the author of a successful novel, was too stunned to speak. I called "Lunch!" and put my arm across his shoulder. Obviously it would be useless to ask him to go on with the scene without giving him a chance to recover. I did my best to calm him down. I told him that the only explanation that made any sense was that one of those parasite yes men who attach themselves to Hollywood greats must have put the bug in Goldwyn's ear during the rushes. I assured the bewildered actor that his performance was excellent—that he should do his best to forget the incident. After lunch we went back to work and that was the last we ever heard of the matter.

Eddie Cantor gave a sterling performance as the emperor's food taster who becomes involved in a conspiracy to poison the current Caesar. A high moment in the show involved getting a laugh through the use of trick photography. Poison has been inserted in all but one of the emperor's favorite delicacies, grilled nightingales. One of the conspirators tells Eddie that the nightingale without the parsley is the one without the poison. To test the truth of this, Eddie tosses a paralyzed bird to Cleopatra, the emperor's pet crocodile. The amphibian swallows the morsel, goes into convulsions, rolls over on his back and becomes rigid. How would you like that for an assignment in direction? We solved the problem by chlo-

Frank Tuttle with (from left) his daughter, Fredrika ("Teddy"), niece, Betty, and daughter, Helen, in Greenwich, Connecticut, 1935.

roforming the crocodile and cranking backwards, which reversed its movements. In other words, what it actually did was gradually to regain consciousness, writhe about, and twist itself onto its feet.

Thanks to Ralph Ceder and his redoubtable stuntmen, the chariot chase came out even better than I had hoped. The close shots of Eddie and his pursuers were shot in process. The moving backgrounds were photographed before we went to work with the principals. Ralph was on hand when we made these studio shots. He had talked the background projectionist into speeding up the moving scenery so that it would match the terrific speed of the action Ralph had already staged. One of the obstacles hit by Eddie's chariot had been a wagon loaded with crates of geese. We tossed a goose onto the floor of Eddie's chariot behind him, whereupon it began to nip Eddie in the derriere. Oddly enough, this was a cinch. We sewed a bright button to the seat of Eddie's tunic. To top this laugh, Ralph introduced a brilliant piece of business on the set. Eddie tucked the goose under one arm and squeezed it. With the help of the sound department we dubbed in a series of honk-honks. The art of the cinema. Yeah, man!

Roman Scandals did better business than any of the previous Cantor comedies. Footnote. Should my readers jump to the conclusion from my account of Mr. Goldwyn's behavior while I was working for him that he is a chiseler, a bully, and a boor, I can only assure them that I have only written exactly what happened. If they believe my recital is unfair, I am sure they can read reams of material which will describe him as a lovable though sometimes eccentric genius. I shall even tell them where to get this material—from the Goldwyn publicity department. One final fact. For weeks after my job was finished, I avoided driving past the Goldwyn studio, because when I did drive by I was seized with an acute attack of nausea. If he remembers me at all, I am sure that Mr. Goldwyn will be delighted to hear this.

CHAPTER 15

Back at Paramount, Cary Grant had now made several pictures, but none of them had given him the chance to show what he could really do. Luckily for me, when I returned to home base, I was assigned to direct Cary in *Ladies Should Listen*, a comedy which would give him an opportunity to display his fine talents in this field for the first time. Douglas MacLean, a star of the silent days, was our producer, and one of his outstanding contributions to the script was to give the dialogue a sophisticated polish. Even to this day few people realize what a gifted comedy writer Douglas is.

Cary's leading lady was Frances Drake. They were aided and abetted by such laugh-getting experts as Edward Everett Horton, George Barbier, and Nydia Westman. *Ladies Should Listen* was a delight to direct and was the first of a long list of sophisticated comedies in which Cary Grant has since become particularly successful, although he is a fine actor in all departments.

Here Is My Heart was a musical version of *The Grand Duchess and the Waiter*, starring Bing Crosby. Rainger and Robin wrote the score, which included a number which is still popular today, "June in January."

The setting for *Here Is My Heart* was Monte Carlo. Bing, playing a popular American singer, masquerades as a waiter to finagle his way into the suite of a Russian noblewoman. Kitty Carlisle, who later married Moss Hart, played the grand duchess. A fine singer, Kitty had vocalized with Bing before in a rendition of Rainger and Robin's "Love in Bloom." Their imperial highnesses the duchess' two brothers were played by Roland Young and Reginald Owen. Among the other fine actors in *Here Is My Heart* were Bill Frawley and Akim Tamiroff.

Lobby card for *Here Is My Heart*, 1934.

 Bing had developed into a first-rate comedian. When he served dinner to the Russians wearing a false moustache, his eyes were fastened on the lovely grand duchess. As a result he knocked over glasses and had to snatch his moustache from the soup. Bing played his broad scene with the telling seriousness of an accomplished farceur.

 Bud Lighton, who produced Harlan Thompson's excellent script, felt that the picture needed an added scene to build up the romance between the grand duchess and the waiter. He engaged playwright Vincent Lawrence, the most gifted pinch hitter in the writing profession. The dialogue he concocted for Bing and Kitty was a minor masterpiece, and they played it to the hilt.

There's a story behind my directing Carl Brisson and Mary Ellis in *All the King's Horses*. Manny Cohen, who had been a successful New York executive, was now the head of Paramount's Hollywood studio. The picture's producer was my old friend, William LeBaron. When Manny told me they wanted me to do the job, I said I was keen about directing John Galsworthy's beautiful short story, *The Apple Tree*. I had bought the film rights from Galsworthy, and he had okayed the screen version I had written. I begged Cohen to read it. He did so and agreed that Galsworthy's story was a literary gem, but was worried about its possibilities for the screen because of its tragic ending. After a lengthy discussion, Manny said he would schedule *The Apple Tree* on Paramount's list of coming attractions, but only on condition that I first direct the Brisson picture. Our agreement, too, had a tragic ending. A few months after we had shaken hands on the deal, Manny left Paramount.

As a nightclub singer, Carl Brisson was the dowagers' darling. A champion Danish boxer, he was a fine figure of a man with a charming smile and dimples already yet! Our story had to do with a mythical kingdom monarch and an actor who looked almost exactly like him—courtesy of special effects and the split screen gimmick. As the actor's agent, Gene Pallette gave his usual diverting performance.

Mary Ellis was then at the height of her career as a musical comedy star, notably as the heroine of *Rose Marie*. Her lovely voice and face were a tremendous asset to the picture. Our composer-lyricist was Sam Coslow, who had recently written "Cocktails for Two," which Brisson had sung in *Murder at the Vanities*. For *King's Horses*, Sam came up with a hit tune, "White Gardenia," the idea for which had been suggested to him by Carl Brisson.

Carl was a great draw as a nightclub performer, but his experience in this métier had got him into this habit of selling a song—projecting it for the nightspot listeners. The scene in which he sang "Gardenia" called for an entirely different approach. Dining alone, the king starts the number by talking the verse and when he sings he must continue the illusion that he is conjuring up a romantic picture for himself. He must never appear to be performing for an audience. Because he had never faced such a problem before, it took Carl quite a while to feel comfortable doing this.

I remember this incident well. It was Christmas Eve and everyone was anxious to call it a day and go home, but our crew was the soul of cooperation. All of them were wonderfully patient and helpful until we got a take that everyone liked. Carl was a good sport about his slowness in delivering what we were after. Several years later we met again in Europe. Carl slapped me on the back and began to apologize all over again. A sweet guy.

When Dashiell Hammett arrived in Hollywood, everyone wanted to meet him. Aside from his unique writing style and the popularity of his books, the fact that the background of his private eyes was based on his own experiences in that field led writers and directors to search him out and question him. His remarks were brief and cynical. He assured us that the major part of a "private richard's" activities was usually a tedious routine which dealt with such dull employers as husbands checking on their wives and similar sordid assignments. In constructing his fictional detective stories, all he had retained was the meticulous methods of the real life investigators. His plots and his characters were his own. From *The Maltese Falcon* to *The Thin Man*, his novels all made hit pictures. I was among the lucky directors who got a crack at a Hammett yarn, *The Glass Key*, in which George Raft and Edward Arnold were starred.

I had heard that Raft was temperamental, difficult, and cursed with such an ungovernable temper that if anyone crossed him, he would knock the offender cold. I soon found out that this was a Hollywood myth. On the contrary, George Raft is extremely sensitive, proud, and honest. He is a hard worker and intensely loyal. He appreciates every constructive suggestion, and once he believes you're his friend, he'll be in your corner for life. He does have a quick temper, but he makes a great effort to control it and succeeds unless he is unbearably provoked. I remember an incident which illustrates this. Because the studio physician was busy, a doctor had been sent for to bandage George's face for a hospital scene. The man was noticeably clumsy, but I was shocked when George suddenly told him to lay off—to beat it. I stepped close and got a whiff of the doctor's breath. He was higher than a helicopter. I got rid of him and we waited for the studio doctor.

Before the picture started, George and I ran over the script together. He indicated the word "point." With characteristic honesty, George told me that he'd been raised in a tough section of Brooklyn where the word was pronounced "pernt." "I can't say 'point,'" he said. I grinned. "You just did," I said. He grinned back at me. We both laughed. Since then we've had a lot of laughs together.

Movie still from *The Glass Key*, 1935, with George Raft, center.

Hammett's story had to do with a political boss, played by Edward Arnold, whose loyal sidekick was George Raft. Arnold was infatuated with the daughter of a distinguished senator played by Charles Richman. The girl considered Arnold a cheap parvenu, beneath her contempt. Walking home late one night, Raft comes upon the senator's son, played by Ray Milland, lying dead in the gutter. He has been beaten over the head by the conventional blunt instrument. When Raft tells Arnold about the murder, the boss' reaction is an indifferent shrug. Raft, and the audience, begin to suspect that Arnold may have killed the senator's son, and later the senator's daughter is convinced that he did.

Robert Gleckler and Guinn (Big Boy) Williams were cast as a gangster and his bodyguard who are working against Arnold and the candidates he is backing. With the idea of getting into the good graces of Gleckler so that he can dig up information that may be helpful to Arnold, Raft stages a phony quarrel with Arnold in front of Gleckler and Williams. But Gleckler finally becomes suspicious and has Williams dump Raft into a secluded tenement room where "Big Boy" periodically beats him unconscious, throws water on his face, and orders him to spill what Gleckler is trying to find out. This scene was taken practically verbatim

A photograph of one of Frank Tuttle's paintings, produced while he was a student of Stanton MacDonald Wright.

from Hammett's novel. It was written with brutal humor. Williams comments that Raft is a "masocrist"—he likes to be slugged, Williams says. When George passes out for the third time, the goons start a card game in the next room. Raft comes to and tries the window. It is locked, so he sets fire to the mattress. When the thugs burst into the smoke-filled room and start stamping out the fire, George crawls out the door, opens a hallway window, drops to a roof and escapes.

The windup of the yarn shows Raft finding the real killer. It is finally revealed that the senator had quarreled with his no-account son and beaten him to death with the metal head of his walking stick.

The Glass Key was so successful that Paramount remade it several years later with Alan Ladd and Brian Donlevy in the Raft and Arnold roles. For me it was a welcome change from the light type of picture I had recently been associated with.

At about this time someone told me that the noted American painter, Stanton MacDonald Wright, was conducting a life class in downtown Los Angeles. During my summer vacation when I was seventeen, I had attended such a class at the Art Students' League in New York, and I had a sudden yen to try my hand again, so I met Mr. Wright and enrolled. I then discovered that my teacher was the brother of Willard Huntington Wright, who, as S.S. Van Dine, had written the Philo Vance mysteries I'd directed.

Wright's class started at 7:00 A.M. and continued until 9:30, at which point we would have devoted a half hour to each of five drawings. Following this, everyone chipped in a dime and we had coffee and crullers. We sat around and talked. Once a week Stan Wright lectured about painting. His teaching also included his moving from student to student and drawing the model himself, explaining what he was doing and criticizing the student's own sketches. It was great fun and Wright's lectures gave us lots to think about. He had an overall theory that the great masters were a product of their times and environment. He believed, for instance, that Cimabue and Giotto were the outstanding painters of the Renaissance because, aside from their talent, their religious beliefs were profound and moved them deeply. Later the culture of the period lost much of its faith and painting deteriorated.

Wright was particularly interested in Chinese painting and sculpture. He used to say that the Chinese creators of those superb horses were not so idiotic as to expect the beholder to think he was looking at a real

Cinematographer Henwar Rodakiewicz confers with Frank Tuttle on the set of *Two for Tonight*, the 1935 film starring Bing Crosby and Joan Bennett, with Mary Boland, Lynne Overman, and Thelma Todd.

horse. He gave the viewer credit for accepting it as the creation of an artist. Wright also believed that the emptiness of a great part of modern art, no matter how brilliant its design and color, was due to the sterility of most of the modern artists who, in this age, believe in practically nothing.

While I was still attending Wright's classes, he was commissioned to paint a mural on the walls of the Santa Monica Post Office. In the group representing motion pictures, Stan's models were Gloria Stuart, Leo Carillo, and I. As far as I know, my map is still among those present.

Another event of this period was the founding of the Screen Directors' Guild. After the organizing of the actors, a number of directors began to talk about our following suit. A few of us had dinner at my house and kicked in a hundred bucks a piece to take care of other meetings at which we could find out how our fellow directors felt about the idea. My guests included John Cromwell, John Ford, Rouben Mamoulian, Lewis Milestone, King Vidor, and William Wellman. After a series of meetings at the Hollywood Athletic Club, we finally organized with King Vidor as our first president, but it took more than a year for the Guild to be recognized by the Producers' Association. Today, the Directors' Guild of America has its own building and theatre and a national membership of over two thousand.

CHAPTER 16

College Holiday was a Paramount musical produced by my good friend, Harlan Thompson, who, you may remember, had written the screenplay for *Here Is My Heart*. This one had the greatest collection of comedians ever assembled on the Paramount lot. Among those present were Jack Benny, Burns and Allen, Martha Raye, Mary Boland, and Ben Blue. The romantic leads were played by Marsha Hunt and Leif Erickson. Eleanore Whitney and Johnny Downs sang and danced subsidiary romantic roles. The crazy-quilt plot was motivated by Mary Boland's search for the "Body Beautiful," for which she had congregated a coterie of collegians. The tale concluded with a show in which the kids did their specialties. The finale was a minuet danced by Gracie Allen, George Burns, and Ben Blue—a real show stopper.

One of Gracie's mad pranks in this conglomeration of music and whoop-de-do was to smack the spooning collegians with marshmallows shot from a blowgun. While we were photographing this sequence, Mr. Cecil B. DeMille was escorting Ambassador Grew around the Paramount lot. The dean of directors introduced me to our distinguished ambassador and indicated what the cameraman was accomplishing in lighting up the set. He explained to Mr. Grew that the process of lighting was similar to the painting of an artist. Considering the nature of the scene that was about to be photographed I couldn't resist adding my two cents worth. "What he is painting, Mr. Ambassador," I said solemnly, "is Miss Gracie Allen smacking actors in the puss with marshmallows!" Mr. Grew was kind enough to give me a sympathetic grin.

The little father of Paramount is Adolph Zukor, one of the pioneers of important picture making in America, and one of the wisest men ever connected with the industry. A small, shy man, Mr. Zukor is often unnoticed as he strolls about on the outskirts of the bedlam which usually precedes the taking of a shot. One day he beckoned me aside and asked me to do him a favor. He explained that *College Holiday* would triple its take if we could get it into the theatres for Christmas week. Did I think this was possible? I said I thought we had a chance if I could engage a second unit director in whom I had great confidence to stage several of the musical numbers for us. Naturally I would always make a quick visit to his set when he was ready to go and watch a final rehearsal. Zukor assured me he would get the man I wanted and do everything else he could to help. The director I had in mind was Henwar Rodakiewicz, a Harvard graduate who had made several remarkable documentaries and had been on my staff during the shooting of *The Glass Key*. He was available. We got him and he did a wonderful job. The picture was in the theatres Christmas week.

There is a tendency among certain directors, writers, and actors, to have a rather superior attitude toward the front office. They seem to feel that desk jobs are handled by stuffed shirts who contribute practically nothing and waltz off with a fat percentage of the profits. Possibly there is some justification for this point of view, but I have become more and more convinced that the making and selling of motion pictures is such a complicated operation that all of us who are involved in the process can be real contributors to the final result. It seems to me that everyone who helps get a winner up there on the screen should be judged by his merits. I am sure that no one would deny that Adolph Zukor's contribution to the success of Paramount's pictures has been enormous. When *College Holiday* began to clean up he came to me and told me he would arrange for me to take a three-month holiday on salary, but my respect for Adolph Zukor is based on more than his generosity.

Waikiki Wedding was the most successful of all the pictures I made with Bing Crosby. Arthur Hornblow was its producer and the cast included Shirley Ross, Martha Raye, Bob Burns, George Barbier, Leif Erickson, Anthony Quinn, and many other fine performers. The score was by Rainger and Robin and included "Sweet Leilani" by Harry Owens, whom Bing had met in Hawaii. LeRoy Prinz staged the dances with the help of Mrs. Beamer, a native of the hula.

If you happened to see *Waikiki Wedding*, you may be interested to learn that the whole picture was shot on Paramount's sound stages with the exception of a few chase long shots which were photographed with doubles on the beach at Waikiki. The illusion that it was shot on location was accomplished by the ingenuity of the set designers and constructors, who built an entire Hawaiian village on one of the sound stages with an amazing realistic sky backing. All this was beautifully photographed by Karl Struss, whom I had known since the days when he sold still photographs to Frank Crowninshield at *Vanity Fair*.

Bing played a press agent who had hit upon a publicity stunt for his pineapple-canning boss, played by George Barbier. Bing figured that the stunt would allow him and his pal, Bob Burns, to spend most of their time fishing and swapping yarns. Bing's idea was to present a free trip to Hawaii to Shirley Ross, a contest winner who would then, Bing hoped, sing the praises of the islands. The flaw in this great scheme was that Shirley found Hawaii to be a big bore and said so, which left Bing holding the bag. Now he had to convert the contest winner to the charms of Honolulu or be fired. Desperate, he finally came up with a solution. He would personally conduct Shirley on a sightseeing tour to an obscure outlying island. This, he assured his boss, would do the trick.

Guided by a native pal of Bing, played by Tony Quinn, the expedition stumbles into one series of adventures after another. The plot is further complicated by romance rearing its happy Hawaiian head. Bob Burns, too, becomes involved with Martha Raye, who, I soon discovered was one of the all-time greats among comediennes and a real darling.

Shirley falls for the whole bit including Bing, but when they return she uncovers the trick Bing has played on her. She is furious. Boy loses girl; but in the end Don Hartman and Frank Butler, our writers, arranged it so that love laughs at their plot reversals and conquers all—in time for the final fadeout.

In the staging of Bing and Shirley's rendition of the Rainger-Robin hit tune, "Blue Hawaii," I interpolated something in its staging which I felt quite happy about. I had always been annoyed by performers being letter-perfect in the words of a song when they've obviously never had a chance to learn them. Our scene took place on Bing's sailboat. A group of native sailors is stretched out in the prow, singing the number in Hawaiian. Bing sings the English version and asks Shirley to try it, but before she sings each line he talks the lyrics. I felt that his casual approach would help our audience to believe the scene was really happening.

Like all musicals, *College Holiday* and *Waikiki Wedding* were pretty complicated to shoot, so that I only directed two pictures that year. One of the trade papers published a list of directors whose movies had taken in the most shekels that year. I was delighted to find that my name was second only to Frank Capra's on the list.

Upon my return from the European vacation I took, kindness of Adolph Zukor, I directed two more musicals starring Bing. The first of these, *Dr. Rhythm*, gave Bing and me one of the biggest kicks of our careers. His co-star was Beatrice Lillie. We were both fans of this superb comedienne and we had a ball working with her. Several years before this, Bea had attended a party I'd given for Florence Vidor and Jascha Heifetz. Another guest was Charlie Chaplin, whom I'd previously met at King Vidor's. After dinner he started clowning around with Bea. The astonishing feature about this was that the great Chaplin played straight for her. While he was doing an impersonation of an Italian tenor, Bea, with devastating deadpan dignity, began to go through his pockets and ended up on the floor, her ankles twined around the tenor's neck.

Dr. Rhythm was suggested by an O. Henry short story and adapted for the screen by Jo Swerling and Richard Connell. The opening sequence they developed was so wonderfully mad that I'll summarize it briefly. A doctor, Bing, a policeman, Andy Devine, the driver of a Good Humor wagon, Sterling Holloway, and a zoo attendant, Rufe Davis, meet mysteriously in Central Park. We soon discovered that in their youth, they were the members of P.S. 162's championship relay team. After singing the class song, they stripped to their underwear and restaged the race around the seal pool. Food and drinks follow and they get amiably potted. The policeman dives into the pool and is bitten in the behind by a resentful seal, whereupon Andy bites him back.

This creates a dilemma. Andy has an appointment in the morning with Bea Lillie, whose niece, played by Mary Carlisle, has taken up with a scheming fortune hunter (Fred Keating). Because the seal's bite had rendered him *hors de combat*, Andy begs Bing to masquerade as a copy and keep the date for him. Bing agrees and Dr. Rhythm is on his way.

The score for *Dr. Rhythm* was written by Jimmy Van Heusen and Johnny Burke, two of the best. Our cameraman was Charles Lang. I shall never forget something this fine photographer taught me during the evening shoot. I had prepared what I thought was a beautifully composed set up, but when I showed it to Charley he shook his head and pointed to the background. "What's happening back there is funny," he said. "Your fancy foreground will kill the joke." How right he was. The smarty-arty foreground was removed.

The second unit cameraman was Floyd Crosby, who had won an Academy Award for shooting Murnau's *Tabu*. At the time he joined us, Floyd's pictures had all featured exteriors. Charley Lang took an instant liking to him and gave him some shrewd tips about working indoors. Another contributor to the success of *Dr. Rhythm* was Herb Polesie, who worked as an advisor on story construction and picture planning.

Working with Bea Lillie was a constant delight. We had only one argument and the basis for that was rather curious. In the story an adjustable table in the doctor's office gets out of control and spins Bea violently around. Her next scene was with Andy Devine and I suggested she would get some additional laughs if she dizzily jerked her head when she talked to him. Bea didn't want to do this because, she explained, she had always been most effective when nothing disturbed her equanimity. I saw her point, but I felt sure that, after what she'd been through, her failure to be composed despite her belief that she *was* the height of dignity would be both right and funnier. She was frankly skeptical, but she finally agreed to try it my way. Next day, when we saw the rushes, she graciously patted me on the back and agreed that her fears had been groundless.

Another highlight in the show was an operetta at the policemen's ball, in which Bea did a travesty of a coloratura, and Bing appeared as a mustachioed ballet dancer. Believe it or not, Bing, who is a born athlete, leaped into the air and did a couple of entrechats. I believe that Bing was prouder of this accomplishment than of winning an Academy Award for his performance in *Going My Way*.

As we had hoped, Bea's unique delivery of songs and comedy scenes was hailed with delight across the nation, and Bing, too, gave a fine comedy performance. We had a hit.

Harlan Thompson was my producer when Bing did *Paris Honeymoon*. The script was by Frank Butler and Don Hartman, who later became the head of production at Paramount.

Bing's leading lady was the Hungarian actress, Franciska Gaal. This young lady was something of a problem. When she was very young, she had been a European star. Now she was at the age where her determination to be a teenage cutie impelled her to bounce around at the slightest excuse. I seldom bawl people out, but in this case I finally had to. I took her aside and told her that what she was doing was what golfers call "pressing." She was forcing everything, which hurt her performance and made her actions seem unbelievable. I told her to simplify her approach. I added that if she would concentrate on the content of her scenes instead of thinking about herself, she would be doing this picture and herself a great service. She reacted like a spoiled child who has just been paddled. She pouted and said I was absolutely right and that she would do what I had told her to; and she did try, but she remained an *enfante gatée* to the end. Bing used to play his songs with her with this usual skill and charm, but the moment I said, "Cut!" he would walk away.

Bing played an American rancher, engaged to Shirley Ross, who is determined to sandpaper his rough edges. As they have agreed, he follows Shirley to Paris and they finally end up in a small town somewhere in the Middle East. As the local innkeeper, Akim Tamiroff explains to Bing, in the early summer, when the rose festival is in progress, "the whole place stinks!"

The plot involves a haunted castle which Bing takes over, accompanied by this man played by Edward Everett Horton. When the housekeeper is taken ill, her niece shows up to help. The niece is Franciska Gaal.

My being accessible and easy to talk to was responsible for an amusing piece of business which was suggested by our prop man. The incident took place in a deserted shack where Bing and Franciska have taken refuge when Bing's car breaks down. Following a spat, Bing tells Franciska to stay on her side of a line he has drawn on the dirt floor with a pickaxe. They are both famished. A hen scurries into the shack. They get down on their hands and knees and crawl after the hen as it retreats, walking on the line. When it reaches the rear wall, they grab it.

While we were preparing the setup, the prop man whispered, "Frank. Crank backwards!" Busy with the usual fiddling around that accompanies getting ready for a shot, I nodded, hardly conscious of what he had said. Then it hit me. If the couple backed away from the hen with something edible in their hands, the hen would follow them, and if we cranked backwards it would appear to be *backing* away from them. Done the prop man's way, the scene was one of the biggest laughs in the picture.

Naturally everything ends happily for Franciska and Bing. The conclusion of this musical coincided with the end of my Paramount contract, and I decided not to renew it. I felt that now I was really going to be typecast as a director of musicals, and that I must get away from even Crosby musicals or I'd end up humming my way into oblivion.

Before long, my agent got me a job at Universal. The picture, *I Stole a Million*, starred George Raft and featured Claire Trevor. Claire and George worked together beautifully, and she and her husband, Milton Bren, became good friends of mine. George has a great respect for top performers and is inclined to run himself down as an actor. I saw *I Stole a Million* recently on TV and, if you saw it too, I'm sure you'll agree that his acting was excellent.

Nathaniel West wrote an excellent screenplay. Shortly after the picture was released, "Pep" West was killed in an automobile crash. I believe his novel, *The Day of the Locust*, will be remembered for many years as a revealing picture of life among Hollywood's obscure bit players and hangers-on. *I Stole a Million* told of the struggle of a taxi driver—George Raft—to earn enough to support his wife—Claire Trevor—and child. After a long series of reverses he becomes desperate and is talked into helping in a robbery. Once the underworld characters have their hooks in him, he can't shake them loose. Robbery follows robbery and he is constantly on the lam. Finally his wife meets him in a deserted shack and pleads with him to give himself up. Faced with this alternative or the life of a hunted criminal, he surrenders to the police.

Dick Foran, as the wife's faithful friend, and Victor Jory, as the underworld character who started Raft on his criminal career, were among the fine actors in our supporting cast.

Despite the success of *I Stole a Million*, my determination not to do any more musicals made it difficult for my agent to find a spot for me. While he was making the rounds, Universal, where the Raft picture had been shot, asked me to direct an Edgar Bergen comedy, *Charlie McCarthy, Detective*. Hoping this would give us additional time to dig up the right picture, I said yes.

I had a high regard for Mr. Bergen, and the story idea they were considering sounded as though it could be developed into something quite unusual. Unhappily the time needed to prepare what I had liked forced them to abandon the original idea, so they whipped up a more or less conventional whodunit with Louis Calhern as the victim and Robert Cummings as a charming friend of Bergen who turns out to be the killer. Doing the picture did have its compensations however; it had Edgar Bergen, Charlie McCarthy, Mortimer Snerd, and "slow burn" Edgar Kennedy as a bumbling detective.

The special delight of working with Edgar Bergen was his use of Charlie between shots to comment on the people around them with sardonic wisecracks. Bergen's skill with Charlie is so amazing that you find yourself treating Charlie as though he were a live person. Bergen had some trouble with the dialogue in one scene and Charlie blew his lines seven times. For fear of compounding whatever was bothering Edgar, I said nothing. Charlie looked up at Bergen and said pathetically, "Bergen—Do you think Mr. Tuttle will ever hire us again?" I was too stunned to answer. *Charlie McCarthy, Detective* was nothing to write home about, but working with the two great Edgars, Bergen and Kennedy, was great fun.

CHAPTER 17

Remembering that the good Lord helps those who help themselves, I now began to devote all my time and energy to searching for that elusive top story property. My spade work finally led me to my friends in Paramount's story department. I asked if Paramount owned anything which they had never made because of some problem in the story no one had been able to solve. William Dozier's assistant, Meta Reis, unearthed a novel by the British author, Graham Greene, which, she said, fitted this category. She let me take it home to read.

This Gun for Hire was precisely what I'd been looking for. Certain political aspects of the novel made it obvious why Paramount had been afraid to tackle it. I wrestled with the dilemma for several days before I came up with a solution which I thought might fix everything. I wrote a one-page summary of my solution and presented it to Buddy DeSylva, Paramount's new production head. He liked what I'd done and asked Bill Dozier to find a writer to work with me in preparing a treatment. Dozier suggested Albert Maltz, who had recently won the O'Brien short story award. We went to work.

Albert Maltz had an interesting method of working which, he told me, he had figured out because he didn't trust his memory. He sat at a large, flat-topped desk on which were loose sheets of paper, dozens of pencils, and a stack of folders labeled *Dialogue, Character Backgrounds, Plot Structure,* etc. During our discussions, he scribbled down everything that was said on separate sheets of paper, and at the end of the day our secretary typed these notes and filed them away in the category folders. In this way we never lost any point that had come up, and when we finally wrote our treatment the material was all there and easy to assemble.

Lobby card for *This Gun for Hire*, 1942.

Before we began to write, we had already decided, with Buddy DeSylva's approval, to transform Graham Greene's story from London to Los Angeles. Our first problem was that Raven, Greene's professional killer, had a harelip. In the novel, this worked perfectly because the shocked reaction of people to the deformity made Raven hate them; but in real life a harelip causes its possessor to talk in a peculiar way which, on the screen, could provoke thoughtless laughter. The obvious solution would have been to have given Raven a repulsive facial scar, but Joan Crawford had just appeared in a film with a horribly marked face. We were finally forced to invent an incident in Raven's youth which, we felt, might account for his hating people, particularly women. We would explain that Raven, whose father had been hanged and whose mother had killed herself, had been left in the care of a hateful woman who had beaten him savagely for every tiny transgression. She had finally caught him stealing a piece of chocolate and had smashed his wrist with a flatiron. His misshapen wrist would be a constant reminder of this evil woman.

Our treatment opened with Raven, beset by nightmares, waking up in his shabby room. He picks up a briefcase, studies a printed address, and shoves an automatic into the case.

We pick him up entering a decrepit apartment building. On his way upstairs his progress is blocked by a crippled child, who is sitting on the stairs, playing jacks. She drops her ball and asks Raven to pick it up. Obviously disturbed because the little girl has noticed him, he gives her the ball and goes on up. There is a chain across the interior of the door on which he knocks, but the man who peers at him through the narrow opening lets him in when he identifies himself. Raven gets another shock when he sees a cheap-looking floozy seated on a couch. The man introduces her as his secretary and sends her into the kitchen to brew some tea. After vaguely discussing their deal which seems to have something to do with blackmail, the man extends his hand. Smiling, Raven reaches into his briefcase, whips out his gun and shoots the man dead. The "secretary" appears. Raven mutters, "You shouldn't have been here," and moves toward her. Terrified, the girl runs back into the kitchen, slamming the door behind her. Raven shoots through it twice. We hear her groan and fall. Raven checks that she is dead, searches the blackmailer's desk, finds a paper with some kind of chemical formula on it, and leaves.

Now we discover that Raven has been hired by a Mr. Gates—Laird Cregar—who is working for a mysterious higher-up. Cregar pays off Raven with a roll of ten-dollar bills. When he asks Raven how he feels after a killing, Raven tells him coldly that he feels fine.

Cregar calls on a police lieutenant—Robert Preston—and reports a robbery at the Los Angeles chemical works where he is employed. He gives Preston the serial numbers of the stolen bills—which we realize will incriminate Raven—and leaves. Preston's girl in San Francisco is a singer-magician, Veronica Lake. She auditions for Cregar who has an interest in a Los Angeles nightspot. He hires her. Following the audition, Veronica's agent introduces her to a Congressman who wants her to work as a private investigator for him. He heads a committee which is trying to get the lowdown on the higher-up behind Cregar. She agrees to help him, whereupon he cautions her not to let anyone know what she's doing—not even her detective boyfriend, Bob Preston.

In a train en route to Los Angeles, Raven takes the empty seat next to Veronica. Later, as the train is pulling into Los Angeles, Raven catches a glimpse of Cregar and a squad of police on the platform. He makes a bundle of his coat and Veronica's scarf. When they step off the train they appear to be a married couple with their infant child and elude the police. Before they separate, Veronica tells him she is appearing at Cregar's nightclub. Raven persuades her to meet him outside the place so that he can get to Cregar and force him to reveal the identity of the higher-up. Motivated by her assignment to find out who this mysterious man is, she agrees.

So that night, with Veronica in tow, Raven gets into the club, but Preston intercepts his attempt to confront Cregar. Using Veronica as a shield, Raven makes a quick getaway. The chase that follows winds through the labyrinthine structure of a gasworks and forces Raven and Veronica to take refuge in an abandoned railroad car close to the tracks. Directed by the pursuing Preston, the police surround the vast area of the railroad yard and play their powerful searchlights upon the place. Hidden in the car, Raven opens up and talks about himself, even to the point of giving Veronica a gruesome recital of the incident where the woman smashed his wrist. Instinctively playing the part of an amateur psychologist, she tries to explain that what he has told her is the cause of his hatred of people. Patiently she pleads with him to transfer his determination to revenge himself on the man behind Cregar into forcing the higher-up to confess what is behind his machinations. Raven agrees to do what she wants, but it is obvious that revenge and hatred are still driving him.

In the morning he manages to elude the police long enough to start across the long bridge which spans the railroad yard. A second squad of police appears at the far end of the bridge. Caught between the police who have followed him and the newcomers, Raven jumps into one of the open boxcars of a passing train and escapes. Preston finds Veronica in the abandoned car and third degrees her into revealing that Raven is headed for Cregar's office.

At the chemical works a gasmask drill is in progress. Raven steals a mask and puts it on. He confronts Cregar and forces him at gunpoint to take him to the higher-up, who, we learn is the head of the chemical plant—an ancient schemer played by Tully Marshall. With the help of Marshall's long-suffering male nurse, Raven gets the old man to sign a confession that he has been selling poison gas to the Japanese at a tremendous profit. Cregar reaches for a gun and Raven kills him. Meanwhile Preston has led the police to Tully Marshall's office. They cut through the steel door with blow torches, while Preston lowers himself to the office window on a painters' scaffold. The police burst in and shoot Raven, but he dies knowing that he has got the confession for the only person he has ever trusted.

Naturally the names of the actors who eventually played the various roles were not in the treatment we submitted to Buddy DeSylva, but something else was. While we were working on the story, I dropped into the office of Paramount's location department and asked them to give me a list of all the out-of-the-way spots in Los Angeles which, for one reason or another, they'd never been able to use. They were delighted to do this and came up with the gas works, the railroad bridge, and most picturesque of all, the abandoned car which not only existed but was actually occupied by a family of squatters.

At all events, DeSylva liked what we'd written and made several excellent suggestions for changes. Then, from left field, he suddenly let me have it. It was a shame, he said, but of course I couldn't direct the picture. I was strictly a *Waikiki Wedding*-type feller. For a bad ten seconds I was too stunned to utter a word. Then, as Ray Griffith used to say, Saint Anthony came down and whispered in my ear. I asked Buddy if he'd ever seen *The Glass Key*. "Of course," he said. "Fine picture. Who directed it?" When I told him that I had, he was as stunned as I'd been. See what I mean by typecasting? Never mind. I got the job.

We went to work on the screenplay and Paramount went to work trying to find a name actor to play Raven. Not one male star who suited the role was available, so Bill Meiklejohn, the head of Paramount's talent department, suggested a young actor he thought would be great and who was represented by Sue Carroll. Just previous to this, Miss Carroll had abandoned her successful acting career and become an agent. The actor's name was Alan Ladd.

The moment Alan read for me, I was sure we'd found our Raven, but the part was so important that I asked DeSylva to let me make a really thorough test. He told me to go to it. I prepared a series of scenes because, in addition to verifying how right Meiklejohn was, I was anxious to convince Buddy that I was the guy to direct that show. I wanted to bury that "director-of-musicals" tag once and for all. Veronica Lake was working so I selected Pamela Blake, a fine actress who was later okayed by producer Richard Blumenthal for the part of the slatternly maid, to play the scene with Raven, where he tells her how his wrist was smashed. To further ensure the test I secured John Seitz to photograph it. As a result John was assigned to the picture. Perhaps the most curious fact about

Alan Ladd, an early publicity photograph.

This Gun for Hire was that, despite an enthusiastic press, the lack of star names weakened the picture's drawing power the first time around, but the reruns chalked up a record score at the box office. By then, of course, the audiences had had a chance to see Alan in a second picture.

Shortly after the release of *Gun*, Sue and Alan were married and over the years, they have never stopped telling the world that I was responsible for his becoming a top money star. In every conceivable way they have continued to be my close and wonderful friends. Of course the simple truth is that Alan's success was due to one person—Alan Ladd. If you like,

Frank Tuttle with his daughter, Helen, poolside in Hollywood, 1942.

my using him was a lucky break for Alan, but the luck was mine too, just as it was Bill Meiklejohn's and Paramount's.

This Gun for Hire was made about twenty years ago. At the risk of seeming to pat us all on the back, when it turns up on the late show from time to time, it's still a hell of a picture.

As soon as the United States entered the war, the motion picture industry joined with the rest of the nation in the struggle to defeat Nazi Germany and her "honorary Aryan" ally. Aside from the Hollywood men and women in the armed forces (as a director my mind naturally remembers immediately George Stevens, Frank Capra, William Wyler, and many others), the movie people showed up at the Hollywood Canteen to entertain service men and produced training films and other short subjects requested by the military. One of the most interesting contributions was a series of live plays which were motored to camps not too far from Hollywood where they were presented by the Hollywood Actors' Lab in collaboration with the U.S.O. During the week various directors rehearsed these shows at night, since many of the volunteer actors were involved in picture work during the daytime. Our trips were made to the camps on weekends. We rehearsed two sets of actors so that if anyone were ill or on location, a substitution could be arranged and a full cast made available. Our scenery was limited to drapes, furniture, and properties.

For our show, *The Male Animal* by Elliott Nugent and James Thurber,

Tuttle's second wife, Tatiana ("Tania") with their daughter, Barbara, 1942.

one of Paramount's ablest set designers, Bernard Herzbrun, sketched a stage plan which was sent to the camp a week before we arrived so that our stage was all set up when we got there. We also brought along a one-girl Greek chorus in the shapely shape of Shelley Winters, whose career was just starting. Shelley appeared before every act with some amusing chatter written for her by a top Paramount comedy gagman. As you can imagine, the audience cheered and whistled when Shelley appeared, whereupon she said, "Gee, it's wonderful appearing before this kind of an audience—I mean you still have your teeth to whistle through!" When the yaks died down, Shelley told the boys that our cast included Hume Cronyn, Neil Hamilton, Jeff Donnell, and other fine actors. During our rehearsal period, Elliott Nugent's understudy showed up (Elliott had played the lead on Broadway). He remembered every piece of business in the original production—a terrific time-saver for all of us.

Before *The Male Animal,* all the plays sent to the camps had been strictly laugh-getters without a serious thought in them, but the Thurber-Nugent play did have a slight point of view aside from its kidding the prominence given to football over education by certain members of the alumni. The young professor (played by Hume Cronyn in the camp production) has read his students a letter written by an anarchist, Bartholomew Vanzetti, to illustrate how feeling and emotion can be put down in broken English and still be more effective than "slick" writing. When he refuses to stop reading the letter, he is threatened with expulsion. His wife, who is not at all an intellectual, stands up for him, and so does the whole faculty. The professor finally wins his point that students have the right to hear all kinds of opinions—that this is part of the American creed of free expression. But of course the reason for the play's Broadway success—and its success at the camps—was its enormously funny scenes.

We presented *The Male Animal* in a great variety of camps—on a tiny stage in a camp hospital, before bath-robed men in wheelchairs, and in a gigantic auditorium which seated more than five thousand men. These performances were all wonderfully rewarding. Many of the servicemen we played to had never seen a play. It was a terrific kick to hear thousands of American fighting men shake the rafters with their cheers and laughter. Without any question it was one of the highest moments in my life.

CHAPTER 18

My next picture—with Alan Ladd—was *Lucky Jordan*, a comedy melodrama. Freddy Kohlmar was the producer and the fine cast he assembled included Helen Walker, Mabel Paige, Marie McDonald, Sheldon Leonard, and Lloyd Corrigan.

Alan played a gangster who is drafted. He hires a gin-loving old lady—Mabel Paige—to be his dependent mother, but the dodge fails. At camp he runs into Helen Walker as a U.S.O. girl. She brushes off his attempts to date her, but he manages a clever escape from camp, taking Helen along as a hostage, together with a briefcase, which holds top-secret information. Back at Lucky's headquarters, his number one boy, played by Sheldon Leonard, has taken everything including Lucky's current moll (Marie McDonald). Leonard reads about the missing briefcase and what it contains. He decides to locate Lucky and steal the top-secret documents which he's sure he can sell for big dough to some Nazi agents he knows. But when Leonard catches up with Jordan and Helen, Lucky hides the briefcase in a hollow tree and knocks Leonard cold. He recovers the case, parts company with Helen, and goes to Mabel Paige's flat to hide out, stashing the briefcase in a hole in the wall. It is Mother's Day, so for laughs, Lucky has brought Mabel a quart of gin; but her reaction is that her "son" has given her the tenderest of gifts, and her eyes fill with tears as she takes a long swig. Mabel and Alan played this scene so convincingly that audience sniffed back a tear or two while they were smiling.

Lucky goes to check around town on Sheldon Leonard's activities, and when he returns he finds that Mabel has been brutally beaten, but she whispers that she told them nothing about where the briefcase is hidden. Lucky steps to the wall to retrieve it and is blackjacked. When he comes to, the case is gone. Pausing only long enough to call a doctor for Mabel, he dashes to his headquarters and gets a hint from Marie McDonald as to the possible whereabouts of the top-secret papers.

In the search that follows, we watch Lucky pick up the trail until he traces Leonard to the estate of a distinguished gentleman who is secretly working for the Nazis (Miles Manders). Manders is cross-examining Helen Walker in his greenhouse. Lucky finally manages to recover the briefcase, but in the chase which ensues, is finally caught and imprisoned with Helen Walker, whom we have seen make a telephone call just before her capture.

The situation is now taken over by a Nazi agent, recently arrived from Germany and brilliantly played by John Wengraf. Aided by Sheldon Leonard and a strong-arm enforcer, Wengraf supervises their giving Lucky a thorough working over to persuade him to reveal the whereabouts of the documents. In all his experiences with rival gangsters Lucky has never encountered such terrible and fiendish devices as the Nazi directs them to use, but he doesn't crack. When he passes out, the hoods go outdoors to follow up a hint they think he has dropped, leaving a German thug with a shotgun on guard.

When he regains consciousness, Lucky signals to Helen to expose one of her legs for the benefit of the guard, who gradually becomes bug-eyed. Lucky snatches the shotgun. The Federal men who Helen had called turn up and grab the conspirators. Helen assures Lucky that she is sure her account of his heroism will get him off with a light sentence. They might even—.

Actually Tunberg and Ware ended the picture with a surprise twist. Back at the camp from which Lucky escaped, someone is indeed being decorated, but it is not Lucky. Instead we find him digging a ditch. Still impenitent, he tosses a shovelful of dirt on his drill sergeant's foot.

The Hour Before the Dawn was the first picture produced by William Dozier, who had been the head of Paramount's story department for several years. Bill was an able executive and an understanding producer to work for. Based on a Somerset Maugham novel, *The Hour Before the Dawn*, in which Franchot Tone and Veronica Lake played the leading roles, told the story of a British pacifist in wartime England who is in love with an Austrian-born refugee. In my opinion, Franchot is one of the outstanding actors in America and a highly intelligent man. We became fast friends. Veronica played one of her most difficult roles as the Austrian girl, and she worked like a Trojan with a German-speaking actor to acquire an authentic accent.

Lobby Card for *The Hour Before the Dawn*, 1944.

When World War II breaks out, Franchot's father, played by that fine English actor, Henry Stephenson, and Franchot's older brother, played by John Sutton, expect Franchot to recant and abandon his pacifist beliefs, but he refuses to do this, although he is willing and anxious to serve his country in any non-military capacity. His unpopular stand takes him to an out-of-the-way farm.

The lovely and talented Binnie Barnes played John Sutton's wife, who had been a showgirl before her marriage. *The Hour Before the Dawn* was shot during the war, so we went to Arizona to photograph our exteriors, because the final episode of the story called for some explosions and we had to go to the wide-open spaces to stage them. Friends of mine who saw the picture have asked me how we were able to make Arizona look like the English countryside. Our set designer solved this by finding a small hill and constructing a British farmhouse on its crest. I've already explained what a glass shot is, and we used this device, painting a British landscape on the glass so that the long shots of the house gave it the appearance of being surrounded by the typical rolling countryside of rural England.

One night after we'd finished shooting, our troupe visited an establishment whose gambling was legal. I noticed how "hep" and successful Binnie Barnes was at the tables. I had also watched her playing gin rummy games with John Sutton, an excellent player, and she usually won. I asked her about her talent at games of chance and discovered that she had once been the only woman in a group which met once a week to play table-stakes poker. Binnie told me the names of some of the men she had played with and I remember that they were all Bat Mastersons. I asked her how she had done at the end of this three-year hitch. "When we quit," she said modestly, "I was $50,000 ahead." Wow! In addition to her beauty and her variety of talents, Binnie Barnes was a wonderful person and the best of good company.

As the Maugham story progresses, it gradually discloses that the Austrian girl, who has now married the pacifist, is a dedicated Hitler-ite. The climax comes when she signals to Nazi air raiders by setting fire to a haystack. Unaware of his wife's role, Franchot hurries home to try and save her from the bombing. Meanwhile, the concussion from one of the explosions has knocked Veronica unconscious. En route to the farm, Franchot stumbles upon the evidence of his wife's duplicity. As she is staggering to her feet, he bursts into the room and accuses her. Her answer is to turn upon him with a Lueger and back toward the stairway. When he follows her up the stairs, she shoots him and runs into the bedroom. Wounded and unarmed, Franchot staggers after her and kicks in the door.

The episode just before this has shown flight commander John Sutton assembling the mass of proof that the Austrian girl is an enemy spy. Now he arrives at the farmhouse and flings open the door. His brother sways painfully down the stairs and reveals that he has killed his country's enemy.

The Hour Before the Dawn was an effective and successful wartime melodrama.

CHAPTER 19

Hostages, my next Paramount assignment, was another story dealing with the war, this time with one of its less publicized aspects, the resistance movement in a Nazi occupied country, in this case Czechoslovakia.

Sol Siegel was my producer and our association won my profound respect and admiration for this fine executive. Outsiders are often curious about the producer's function in picture making. In practice it varies greatly with the personality, experience, and capability of the man who holds the job. A few directors, like George Stevens and William Wyler, themselves produce the epics they direct, but most directors are supervised by a producer. Exactly what his function is can best be illustrated, I think, by telling you some of the things Sol Siegel did as the producer of *Hostages*.

In the preparation period his contributions were particularly important. First, he had found the best available writers for this particular story. Then he had discussed with them how he felt the material should be treated, what points should be accented, what characters should be eliminated or added, and what he believed the opening, the middle of the story, and the climax should be like. He told me that he had talked to them only in the most general terms so that they would feel his confidence in their skill, which was genuine. Later, as they sent him pages of the screenplay, he made no comment except to encourage them, since he felt that criticism would be more effective later. On other occasions he had brought writers in for discussion when he felt the structure was wobbly. In a case of this kind he usually invited the writers to his office to straighten out what had been bothering him. Once this was corrected to their mutual satisfaction, the writers went back to work.

While the screenplay is being written, the producer is simultaneously lining up a cast in collaboration with the director. As the script nears

Publicity still from *Hostages*, 1943, with (from left) William Bendix, Arturo de Cordova, and Luise Rainer.

completion, further conferences are held with the set designer, the location people, and other departmental heads. Before going into the producer's role during the actual shooting, it would probably be wise to let you know what *Hostages* was all about.

The chief character in Stefan Heym's novel was a Czech resistance leader, Janoschek. This man actually existed. His unique trait was an assumed garrulous stupidity. In the screen adaptation William Bendix played Janoschek. He is in charge of the men's room in the basement of a café on the Moldau River. In his role of a moronic, servile attendant, he is able to pick up all kinds of gossip and listen to what the Nazi soldiers talk about. He quickly reports what is useful to the leader of the resistance, played by Katina Paxinou.

Another important character in *Hostages* is a Czech collaborationist, played by Oscar Homolka. The two-time Academy award winner, Luise Rainer, played his daughter, Milada. She meets another apparent collaborationist, played by Arturo de Cordova, who seems to be a cynical newspaperman, but is actually a member of the resistance movement. Paul Lukas, who had just finished his starring role in Lillian Hellman's fine play, *Watch on the Rhine*, proved his versatility by playing the leader of the Nazi occupation forces, Rheinhardt.

The assassination of Nazi officials by the Czechs causes Rheinhardt's men to arrest Janoschek and several others present at the café where Janoschek works and hold them as hostages who will be executed unless someone discloses the identity of the Czech patriots who killed the Nazis. Ironically, Rheinhardt's agents have arrested collaborationist Oscar Homolka along with the rest.

In the scene where Rheinhardt questions Janoschek, Bill Bendix did a superb acting job as the stupid men's room attendant, rambling on with endless double-talk until the infuriated Rheinhardt decides the man is a hopeless idiot and sends him back to his menial job. In the men's room a group of Nazi strong men slugs Janoschek until a blow in the stomach causes him to stagger into a small washroom to throw up. Actually the room gives out onto the Moldau River. Janoschek lowers himself into the water and escapes. He finally makes his way to a waterfront shack and meets Katina Paxinou. They start working out a plan to blow up a huge munition dump. During their plotting, a Nazi launch approaches the shack; but a Czech worker dumps a heavy cradle of pig iron on it.

While during the shooting of this scene, we had a distinguished visitor, a classmate of mine, Archibald MacLeish, the Librarian of Congress. Today Archie is known not only for his remarkable contributions to American poetry, but also for his fine play, *J.B.* I hadn't seen him for years and it was an exciting reunion.

Janoschek's escape from the shack forces Rheinhardt to show the Czechs that he is their master. The hostages, including the collaborator, are lined up against a wall and machine-gunned. Oscar Homolka contributed a brilliant piece of business for his death. He figured that such a man would cling to the idea that his being a Nazi supporter would still save him. Just before he is mowed down with the rest, he shouts "Heil Hitler!"

The Berlin big shots decide that Rheinhardt's blunders have made them ridiculous in the eyes of the world, so they send a new man to replace him. When Rheinhardt protests, his successor shoots him and reports his death as a suicide to Arturo de Cordova and Luise Rainer. De Cordova is present in the next room in his role of a newspaperman.

Meanwhile, the munitions dump is blown up. Gordon Jennings of Paramount's great special effects department staged this in miniature. The spectacular dynamiting is watched by Janoschek from his skiff beneath a bridge across which Arturo and Luise walk on their way out of the city to freedom.

During the actual shooting of a picture, the boss is the director, but a fine producer like Sol Siegel is invaluable in anticipating difficulties which may arise and in many other ways. Luise Rainer is a superb actress, but she felt that the part of Milada didn't give her something she could really sink her teeth into. Sol Siegel sensed this and had a talk with her. He explained that *Hostages* was not a story in which the emphasis was on any individual star. It was about the whole resistance movement. He told her that she was playing even her minor scenes as though they were big emotional crises. He begged her to watch this tendency, since it would only hurt her as well as the picture. She took this criticism very well, but I believe she was never very happy about her assignment. However, I think Sol was right. It was the story of the struggle of a whole people, and its audiences accepted it as that.

I'm sure that everyone who has ever worked with Edith Head, the designer for Paramount's leading ladies and stars, will agree with me that she deserves a special award to supplement the many Oscars she has won. The plaque accompanying the award I have in mind would commend her for always designing creations which are appropriate to the character who wears them. Certain Hollywood-style creators sometimes yield to the temptation to compete with Balmain, Dior, and other great French designers, even when the wearer couldn't possibly afford such expensive apparel.

My long experience in making pictures at Paramount has given me the privilege of working many times with Edith Head. She has never failed to contribute brilliantly to the total pictorial value of the finished product. In addition to creating in terms of what the script calls for, she is also extraordinarily sensitive to the individual requirements of every actress. They all adore her and have the utmost confidence in her ability to meet their particular needs. Even when a character has a limited budget, Edith always adds a touch or two to the dress she has shopped for to make it just right for the actress and comfortable to wear.

Statisticians tell us that the female of the species "audience" is more numerous than the male. Certainly she is often the one who selects which picture to see; and while the men may instinctively feel that the stars they are beholding are becomingly clad, the women are likely to be much more analytical and critical. Okay, men. The next time you take your fair lady to the movies, just check on this and see for yourself what eulogies she will bestow on Paramount's Edith Head. And she'll be right. Edith Head is the greatest.

I was delighted with my next assignment, *Don Juan Quilligan*, a picture to be made at Twentieth Century-Fox with William Bendix, Phil Silvers, Joan Blondell, Mary Treen, and Anne Revere. The producer was my old friend, William LeBaron, and the script was being prepared by one of America's finest writers of satiric comedy, Arthur Kober. I was also looking forward to working for the first time with Darryl Zanuck whose brilliant record for making hit pictures had started when he was a writer at Warner Brothers. I was also happy to be making a comedy after the war dramas I'd been directing.

Our story was refreshingly different. As the captain of a barge which travels back and forth between New York and Albany, Quilligan, the character played by Bill Bendix, becomes involved with two young women who remind him of his mother, whom he had adored for her cheerful laughter and her wonderful cooking. In New York it is Joan Blondell's joyous laugh which first wins his attention, and in Albany, Mary Treen's superb cooking appeals to the skipper's inner urges. The even balance of their attractions is observed by Quilligan's mate, played by Phil Silvers. This dual pull at the captain's heartstrings gradually develops to a point where Joan Blondell's tough brothers and Mary Treen's scheming mother begin to urge Quilligan to come across with that small gold band—or else.

Without a doubt, Bill Bendix is one of the most versatile character actors in Hollywood. He can play anything from brutal heavies to bewildered comics. The combination of Bill and Phil was everything you could wish for. The pressure on skipper Quilligan continues. In two adroitly written episodes, he finally marries both the ladies, which to his confused, innocent mentality seems like an eminently satisfactory solution.

But not for long. Anne Revere, as a gossiping friend of the Blondell clan, becomes suspicious that Quilligan has an Albany attachment. This forces the captain and his mate into a desperate attempt to wriggle out of the dilemma. They came up with a doctored photograph, which shows Quilligan's "bad" twin brother standing next to him. And so the disastrous consequences of the skipper's bigamy are postponed. He breathes freely once more.

At this point in the yarn, Arthur Kober introduced a melodramatic complication. Pursued by the police, gangsters have deposited a victim's body in Quilligan's bunk. Bill and Phil worked out a delayed take on the revelation of the corpse—one of those directorial touches with which this director had nothing to do except to use it and thank its creators. In the captain's cabin, Phil is seated at a desk making notations in the log when Bill becomes aware that there is something peculiar beneath the bedclothes. He brings up a limp arm and trembling asks his mate what he is holding. Lost in his work, Phil gives it a quick glance and says, "A hand." To the befuddled Quilligan this casual reply seems to explain the situation quite satisfactorily. It is not until he gets up and moves slowly to the cabin door where Phil joins him that the truth suddenly dawns on them both. They begin to shiver and stutter with fear. I hope my telling it hasn't spoiled their gag.

Don Juan Quilligan's bigamy finally catches up with him and he is brought to trial. Arthur Kober wrote a hilarious courtroom scene in which Phil Silvers' testimony, aimed at clearing his pal of any wrongdoing, only gets him in deeper and deeper. However, the skipper's obvious lack of any evil intention, plus the sudden revelation that one of the marriages had been performed by a phony minister, gets Quilligan off with a light sentence. In two scenes which were both funny and touching, he assures his wives that he'll always be true to them—both!

When the picture was rough-cut and we showed it to Darryl Zanuck. Bill LeBaron and I were greatly impressed by his brilliance as an editor. He pointed out that one sequence really added nothing to the progress of the story. We agreed and dropped it. In the crazy, fascinating business of making motion pictures, you never stop learning. My next job was an independent picture which involved Bing Crosby; but it wasn't a musical and Bing wasn't in it. He was the boss.

CHAPTER 20

James Edward Grant, whose screenplays have headed the list of box office hits for years, had written a story based on the life of one of the most colorful figures in the history of the manly art of mayhem, John L. Sullivan. Jimmy had titled his script *The Great John L.* He had given it to Bing to read, hoping that he might be interested in raising the money to produce it from a group of well-to-do friends. Bing was interested.

When it came to picking a director, Bing paid me the compliment of saying that Leo McCarey and I were his choices, and as Leo was not available I got the job. Bing was my director's dream producer. He showed up only once, the day shooting began. I presented him with a bullwhip and later dubbed him the great absentee landlord.

Jimmy Grant's story started when Sullivan was a youngster in love with Kathy, Barbara Britton, who adored him but objected to his choice of a career because she felt that the Boston strong boy was trying to prove his importance by battering opponents unconscious instead of giving the world a chance to learn about the wonderful, generous, and lovable side of his character. The great John L. resented her criticism as unfair, and they began to drift apart. Neither of them had really understood the drive that was behind her Johnny's ambition—the fact that in Boston, a poor, Irish-American youngster of the late eighteen hundreds was looked down upon by the Beacon Hill aristocrats of the city. John's boyhood pal, Mickey, was played by Lee Sullivan, whose fine Irish tenor later brought him fame in the Broadway musical, *Brigadoon*. Mickey was distressed when Kathy put off marrying his idol.

Gregg McClure was a discovery of Frank Mastroly, who handled the business end of the production, while Jimmy Grant was what we wistfully called the artistic producer. Gregg was built like the Farnese Hercules and ran a physical culture gym. His career as an actor had been pretty sketchy, but we found a way to remedy this. At this time I was making those weekend trips to army camps with *The Male Animal*.

One of the characters in the play was a college football star. To give Gregg McClure more experience and the chance to appear before a responsive audience, I cast him in this part. Before we started shooting, he played the role several times and very well.

Sullivan's career began during the bare-knuckle days. Jimmy Grant's screenplay showed several of these fights, notably one which took place on a barge up the Hudson. His opponent was the giant, Flood, played by George Matthews. Following his defeat by young Sullivan, Flood became the Boston strong boy's staunch friend and attached himself to the coming champ's training staff. Another bare-knuckle fight was staged in a famous New York nightspot, following a dinner attended by New York's café society.

Before this fight starts, the ladies are asked to leave. Otto Kruger, as a famous newspaper editor, escorts his lovely companion from the room. She is a noted musical comedy actress, played by Linda Darnell. Rumors that Sullivan is something to look at, impel the actress to bribe her way to an upstairs hiding place where she can watch the contest. She is obviously impressed by the Boston strong boy's physical appeal. During the coming winter she introduces herself to John L. when street urchins are crowding around him and feeling his biceps. Linda takes the fighter around the park in her hansom. When Kathy turns down her Johnny's proposal once again, the new romance develops and finally culminates with Sullivan marrying the musical comedy star.

Sullivan soon wins the championship and tours Europe. He spends his money right and left and by the time he has made a big splurge in Paris, Wallace Ford, as his manager, tells him the exchequer is close to zero. As they are talking over this calamity in a café, Sullivan is challenged by the manager of a slender young Frenchman who offers to bet a small fortune on the outcome of a contest to take place then and there. What Sullivan doesn't know is that his challenger is the savate champion of France; so for the next few minutes the American is kicked in the chin, the stomach, and the derriere by the bounding French gazelle, who kisses a lady's hand while he is delivering a back kick into the solar plexus of the champ. Groggy but determined, Sullivan finally catches up with the agile Frenchman and knocks him cold.

When the picture was released, this fight was its comedy high spot, largely due to the delightful performance of the savate champion by ballet dancer, Simon Semenoff, whose many effective roles with ballet theatre, particularly in the field of comedy, had enchanted me for a long time, plus the staging of the bout by John Indrisano. Johnny is a remarkable man. An ex-fighter, he became a student of boxing history. He can name the principals and the results of every fight since bare-knuckle days. Today he is Hollywood's outstanding stager of fights for pictures. He works out a fight blow by blow, a routine which the actors learn by heart as though they were doing a dance number. The fighters never touch one another. Instead of taking a punch they snap their heads back. The sound of the blow is dubbed in later. Simon Semenoff was so impressed by Johnny's staging that he told him he should create a boxing ballet. Johnny grinned, removed the inevitable slender cigar from his mouth, and shook his head. "I guess I'll stick to this," he said. In case I didn't make it clear, he staged all the fights in *The Great John L.*

Sullivan, meanwhile, has never gotten Kathy out of his heart. Gradually his marriage founders and begins to go on the rocks. He starts to drink. His wife does everything in her power to help him but nothing works. Finally the actress and Kathy meet in the lobby of New York's Plaza Hotel. In one of Jimmy Grant's finest scenes, Linda introduces herself to Barbara Britton and tells her she is leaving Sullivan.

The great John L.'s spectacular career as a fighter finally comes to an end when he is knocked out by Gentleman Jim Corbett, played by Rory Calhoun. Sullivan gets drunk. Later, his head splitting, he listens to a moving appeal to get hold of himself from his parish priest, played by J.M. Kerrigan. He listens, but his fighting spirit is gone. He sinks lower and lower. Otto Kruger finds him, drunk and disreputable, in a low-grade saloon. The newspaper editor tells Sullivan that his divorced wife is dying of tuberculosis. Sullivan sobers up, gets into his one good suit, and arrives in time for a few last words with his wife before she dies. In the adjoining room, Kruger faces him. His love for the dead woman moves him to denounce Sullivan bitterly and to prophesy that he will come to a miserable end—in the gutter.

Sullivan returns to the saloon. Voices from the past echo in his ears. He snatches a whisky bottle from the bar, hurls it at the mirror and swears he will never drink again.

He keeps his promise—goes on a temperance tour where he makes a moving speech to thousands of listeners in Chautauqua.

Meanwhile Kathy has found Mickey and begged him to take her to Sullivan. She upbraids herself for having thought she could change her Johnny. She had made the mistake many women make, she says. She had loved him the way he was, faults and all. That should have been enough. When she finds him, Sullivan mistakes her motive for coming. He thinks she pities him and tells her to go away.

But time changes this. The picture ends with the marriage of Kathy and the great John L.

My next job offer came from the fabulous King Brothers, who were busy making a name for themselves as the top producers for Allied Artists. Their success had caused considerable comment because they had once been the promoters of pinball machines. The scuttlebutt you heard at Hollywood and Vine was that they were a couple of shrewd operators with plenty of drive but little or no interest in the finer type of motion pictures. I should like to go on record as stating that this appraisal of Frank and Maurice King was far from correct. Working with them was a pleasure. They had a fine script, *Suspense*, written by one of the ablest craftsmen in Hollywood, Philip Yordan. His play, *Anna Lucasta*, had had a long run on Broadway and had been well received by the New York critics.

The star of *Suspense* was Belita, the British-born ice skater, and with her the King Brothers and I automatically entered the realm of art with a capital A. This amazing young lady performed four exciting numbers in the picture. For one of them she worked out her own choreography with our cameraman, Karl Struss. You can still see it on TV. Make a note not to miss it the next time it shows up. Take my word for it, Belita's conception and interpretation of the music composed by Daniel Amphitiatroff is as beautiful and moving as the dancing of artists like Anna Pavlova.

Phil Yordan's story centered around Belita, the star of an ice show, who is married to the impresario of the spectacle, played by Albert Dekker. Joe Morgan (Barry Sullivan), a brash young vagrant from New York, shows up in Los Angeles and talks Dekker into giving him a job, but his new boss tells him he'll have to start at the bottom, selling peanuts.

The ice show's stage manager, Gene Pallette, takes a liking for the newcomer, who is obviously smitten by Belita's striking beauty. Watching the rehearsal of a new stunt in which the ice star leaps through a paper hoop, Joe Morgan suggests that the trick is pretty flat. Now if the hoop

Publicity still from *Suspense*, 1946, featuring (from left) Eugene Pallette, Albert Dekker, and Barry Sullivan.

were a circle of sharp knives! Belita buys the idea, the dangerous jump becomes a popular feature of the act, and Morgan is promoted to the job of assistant to Pallette.

Morgan moves into a hotel where he soon discovers that Bonita Granville, as a discarded girlfriend, has taken the room across the hall. She is hurt and furious when Joe tells her to get lost—their affair is colder than Siberia.

Before long Dekker leaves town to set up a series of performances in a neighboring city. As soon as he's gone the cocky new assistant makes a play for Belita, but despite a whirlwind rush which culminates in his taking her to a romantic nightspot where they rumba together, she will have none of his advances. When Dekker returns, he senses what's going on and proposes that he and Belita take a long overdue holiday. They leave for Dekker's mountain lodge in the snow country. But their vacation is interrupted by the unexpected appearance of Joe Morgan. He explains his visit by having apparently discovered important business papers which his boss should sign. A heavy snowfall forces Morgan to spend the night on a downstairs couch which Belita makes up for him. From an upstairs bedroom doorway Dekker hears enough to sharpen his suspicions as to the real reason for Morgan's visit.

At breakfast the next morning, Dekker suggests that Belita do a little practicing on a nearby lake. He also suggests, with a friendly smile, that Joe Morgan accompany her. While she is warming up while Joe watches her, a shot rings out and a few moments later a landslide starts. Startled, the couple climb up a mountain path and discover that the slide has become an avalanche, which begins to diminish as they watch. Three mountaineers join them and advise Morgan to take Belita back to the lodge, while they search the environs.

At Dekker's cabin, Joe Morgan discovers that a gun is missing from its wall rack. The mountaineers turn up with the weapon and comment that it is strange Dekker should have taken along such a high-powered gun in a region where hunters bag nothing but small game. When the men have gone, Belita and Joe can only assume that Dekker had tried to shoot Morgan and had himself been killed by the avalanche his shot had started.

Back in town, several days after this, Joe and Gene Pallette have found it impossible to get Belita started rehearsing a new show. She has closeted herself in her apartment and refused to see Joe. Gene calls on her and begs her to pull herself together and go to work. She tells him she has become obsessed with the idea that her husband is still alive and has been watching her. Pallette is sure this is all in her imagination and pleads with her, for the sake of the idle skaters, to shake off her hallucination and get back to the ice. She finally promises to start rehearsing.

The new show is a smash and, at the party after the opening, Joe Morgan poses with the star for some news shots, leaving his champagne glass on a table. When he returns, Joe finds an ornate ring of Dekker's in his glass. He accuses Pallette of putting it there as a grim gag, but Gene indignantly denies this and blames Joe's crazy idea on the champagne.

The next night Joe Morgan is working alone in his office. He gets an eerie feeling that someone else is present, but a quick search reveals nothing. Later, when Belita comes upstairs to ask Joe to take her home, she finds him locking a big roll-top desk. His nerves are keyed to the snapping point, but when she questions him he gets control of himself, blames his jumpiness on overwork, and they leave the office together.

The following afternoon Belita learns from Gene Pallette that Morgan has a new flat-top desk and that Joe had ordered the old desk burned.

She broods over this and that night she tiptoes down the basement stairs and peers into the furnace. Suddenly Morgan's voice asks her what she is looking for. A droplight close to the furnace is the only illumination. As Joe joins Belita, his hat brushes the light and starts it swinging. The rest of the scene is played in this weird lighting. Joe finally confesses that the night before in the office Dekker had confronted him with an automatic and threatened to expose him—to have him thrown back into the gutter. In a struggle for the gun Morgan had killed him and stuffed the body into the desktop. Now, Joe says, they must escape to Mexico. She pleads with him to give himself up. He refuses. She tells him she won't inform the police, but that she'll never see him again. As she turns to go, Joe grabs her arm. She twists free and hurries up the stairs.

Before the next night's show, Belita doesn't answer Joe when he tries to talk to her. During her performance a terrible guilty fear grips him that she will forget her promise and betray him. He must find a way to silence her. Alone backstage, he comes face to face with the giant hoop. He touches one of the knives. It slips forward. As he tightens the gadget that holds it in place an idea begins to take form.

Meanwhile the show progresses to the point where Morgan is to follow the stagehands as they propel the hoop onto the ice. He moves out to the arena and calls for silence. As he does every night, he explains that Belita will circle the ice three times and then leap through the Circle of Death. The kettledrums begin to roll and an ominous hush falls upon the spectators. As the speeding ice star whirls past the far end of the arena, Morgan loosens the gadget. With each of Belita's revolutions the released knife jerks forward inch by inch. At the last moment as Belita speeds faster and faster toward certain death, Joe shoves the apparatus aside. The crowd gasps. Joe points out the knife to Gene Pallette and makes a hurried exit. Pallette assures the crowd that the hoop will be made safe and that Belita will make the jump. The spectators wipe their brows and begin to whisper.

Backstage, Joe Morgan encounters a cocky young peanut seller. Ironically Joe warns him not to get any big ideas and strides out of the building. As he moves down the steps leading from the stage door, Bonita Granville steps from the shadows and drills him with an automatic. Inside Belita and Gene Pallette hear the shots. When they appear at the top of the stage-door steps, Joe is lying dead below them and the police are leading Bonita away.

Publicity still from *Swell Guy*, 1947, starring Ann Blyth and Sonny Tufts.

As Gene and Belita stare down at the dead man, the camera moves up to the *Joe Morgan Presents* sign above the ice palace. *Joe Morgan* is extinguished.

In the making of *Suspense*, as I told you, the fabulous King Brothers gave us all the facilities of a big studio super production—except that their skill as producers got our picture on the screen for a fraction of the millions a big studio would have had to spend. Good old overhead and underhand!

CHAPTER 21

My next job took me to Paris. *Time Running Out* was to be made in French as well as in English. The American producer was a white Russian, Victor Pahlen, and the French ditto was another white Russian, Sacha Gordine. I met Pahlen in New York and read the script. It was an exciting melodrama about a post-war American gangster in Paris, but though the idea was excellent, I felt that the screenplay needed a lot more work, and Pahlen agreed with me. I suggested that he read *Armchair in Hell* by Henry Kane, who, I thought, was the perfect writer for the job. Pahlen read the novel and once more he agreed.

Hank Kane is one of the most colorful and talented figures in modern American fiction. A successful lawyer who knew New York like a book—a Manhattan Baedeker—he had taken a long shot gamble, quit his practice, and written a murder mystery, *A Halo for Nobody*. It hit like a Floyd Patterson left hook. Before long the public and the critics were hailing Henry Kane as the heir apparent to the throne of Dashiell Hammett, who had just about abdicated. A few months previous to my signing with Victor Pahlen, I had met Hank and his beautiful wife, Pat, and we had hit it off like Damon and Runyon. A great many of Hank's novels are laid in New York, and the characters in them are lusty, bawdy, and out of this or any other world. The incidents he creates have to be read to be appreciated, but here's one to illustrate the sort of thing he comes up with. A mobster discovers that one of his underlings has been stealing from a slot machine. To make the punishment fit the crime, he feeds the thief quarters until they kill him.

Pahlen had signed that admirable actor, Dane Clark, to play the American hoodlum. We said farewell to Hank and sailed for Paris to prepare and cast the picture. Hank assured us he would work day and night and airmail us a completed script *tout de suite*.

I hadn't seen Paris since before the Nazi occupation. Its recovery had been miraculous and its spirits were rising like a Phoenix from the funeral pyre. I had been told that its tradesmen would be lying in wait to latch onto those American dollars with which the tourist is theoretically loaded. Although my French was strictly sub-Berlitz, I found all the French people I contacted most helpful and kind. In one left bank restaurant where you stand in line until you are ushered to a large table already crowded with earlier arrivals, I struck up an acquaintance with three young Parisians who spoke excellent English and introduced themselves as the three musketeers. They raised their glasses and drank a toast to me as a symbol of the Marshall Plan. They couldn't have been friendlier or more fun to be with.

Boris Levin, who was to direct the French version, had been a cutter for the American company which had made *The Man on the Eiffel Tower*. Together we began to pick locations and to discuss the sets with a young designer, Bertrand, who proved to be an expert set planner and a fine artist. The cast Pahlen and Gordine assembled included Fernand Gravet, a first-rate actor who speaks flawless English. Our leading lady was Simone Signoret.

As you can imagine, working with this superlative actress several years before she won her Academy Award was an exciting experience. Our picture was shot some time before her marriage to Yves Montand, but their romance was in full flower and I had the pleasure of meeting him and seeing one of his performances. I can assure you that what goes on when Bobby Darin, et al., appear in America is a ripple compared to the reception given Montand in Paris. His thousands of fans really raise the roof. And small wonder.

While we were lining things up, Henry Kane had been knocking himself out in New York. We got his finished script in less than three weeks and it was all that I'd hoped for.

We first met Dane Clark, as the gangster, Eddy Roback, when his hoods of all nations drive their cars in front of the French equivalent of the Black Maria which is transporting him across Paris and he escapes. He makes his way to a department store, where he steals a raincoat. On the top floor he picks up a small boy who starts weeping copiously when Roback hustles him down the stairs. Meanwhile Fernand Gravet, as the police chief assigned to the case, starts placing his men at all the store exits. When Roback gets to the main entrance he finds a squad of police questioning the shoppers as they leave the store. Holding the child close to his face, he hands him to a cop, mumbling something about getting his car. Before anyone can check, he is gone.

Our child actor was a delight. I happen to belong to the school of directors who refuses to scare a child to make it cry. I insisted on the casting department finding me a little boy who would act the part. It was a long sequence. The old tricks to produce the sustained weeping we needed just wouldn't have worked. The angel puss they finally found was a real trouper. He loved to act and could turn on the tears at will. When he was all finished, we gave him a brand-new bicycle. That was the only time he really cried. Then he threw his arms around all of us.

Incidentally, when Dane Clark arrived in Paris, he found a startling surprise waiting for him. Producer Pahlen smilingly told him that he would have to perform the French version—in *French*! "But," Dane protested, "I can't speak a word." Victor grinned. "You will," he said. And he did. The trick was accomplished by Dane doing his French scenes in short pieces which he learned with the help of a young Frenchman who spoke excellent English and repeated the dialogue over and over until Dane, who has an excellent ear, could give an almost perfect imitation. Dane's American accent was perfectly acceptable because the character he was playing would have had one. For all that, I took my hat off to Monsieur Dane Clark for his concentrated hard work. He did a fine job. For my money he can act in any language.

Roback's escape from the department store sends the police inspector to the apartment of a one-time girlfriend of Roback, played by Simone Signoret. She tells Fernand Gravet that she hasn't seen the American gang leader for more than a year. In fact she is now seriously interested in a young American newspaperman, played by Robert Duke. While Gravet is questioning her, Simone gets a telephone call from one of Roback's gang. Gravet listens in, but the message is so skillfully worded that the inspector finds nothing incriminating in it and leaves. Actually the cryptic call had told Simone where she can find Roback. He is hiding out in the studio of a photographer with underworld connections, played by Michel André. Simone's sense of loyalty to the man she once loved impels her to persuade the American newspaperman to drive her close to André's studio.

Simone's meeting with Roback awakens enough of her old feeling for the hunted man to make her agree to join him in a search for money to bribe his way to the Belgian border. When Robert Duke tails her to the photographer's place, Roback's gun forces the newspaperman to drive them in his car. Duke is not too hard to persuade because he feels he can act as Simone's protector. Before they leave, Roback clips the photographer, turns on the gas in the kitchen, shoves André's face close to the open jets and takes off. His pleas for money are all turned down. They set out for the border.

Meanwhile, Fernand Gravet has not been idle. With his aids he systematically grills Roback's known associates until his search leads him to the photographer's studio. André has been almost asphyxiated, but his frantic cat, choking from the gas, had scratched his master across the face and Michel had revived sufficiently to force the kitchen door open. Shortly after this, the inspector arrives with his men. They summon the "pompiers." The French firemen apply their special apparatus for resuscitation. André tells the inspector everything he knows. The chase is on.

After a series of close calls with the gendarmes, Roback takes the wheel of Duke's car and drives at breakneck speed through the fog. Before long he careens off the highway and ends over end into a ditch. Miraculously no one is curiously hurt, but the car is completely wrecked. They proceed across the fields on foot.

On the French side of the Belgian border the trio holes up in a deserted warehouse where Roback is met by a half dozen of his followers. Roback's violent character provokes a quarrel between him and Simone. Jealous of her interest in Robert Duke, he smacks her savagely across the face. She runs from the warehouse en route to the nearest railroad station where she knows Roback has already sent Robert Duke, guarded by a French hoodlum. After Simone's departure, Roback checks the gang's supply of tommy guns preparatory to making a run for the border.

As Simone stumbles into the outskirts of the village, she sees a squad of police cars assembling under the direction of Fernand Gravet. She hesitates, torn between her old loyalty and her chance to escape from the hold Roback still has on her. She searches her heart, realizes she cannot run off without warning Roback, and turns back.

In acting out this moment of decision, Simone had some difficulty in finding a way to show what was going on inside. This type of dilemma is quite common with the conscientious, intelligent actor. Simone couldn't force herself to make an unmotivated move. It developed into quite a thing. I was finally able to suggest enough of a motive to satisfy her and we got the shot. It was a curious kind of impasse. We were faced with the unpleasant fact that the situation just had to be resolved or else the conclusion of the story wouldn't play. In a case like this, the actress and the director simply must settle for the best solution they can devise—perfect or not. Thinking it over that night, I remembered something about the incident which amused me. To keep Simone continually in camera range while she was running into the position where she would make her decision, it had been necessary to draw a chalk line to guide her. Naturally she was happy to have the chalk line, but if you wanted to over-intellectualize the move, her motive for running along the line wasn't exactly rooted in the character she was playing. It was a mechanical *necessity*. Motive—schmotive! She just had to use it.

To get back to the story, Simone arrives back at the warehouse before the police. A few moments later, when Gravet shouts to the gangsters to surrender, Roback answers with his tommy gun. The police return his fire, break down the door, and pour into the warehouse. A volley of shots kills Simone, who falls at the top of a long flight of wooden stairs. Above her, Roback empties his machine gun, is riddled by a dozen bullets, pitches forward and falls part way down the stairs, his legs tangled in the outstretched arms of the dead Simone. The picture ends with Robert Duke boarding the train for Paris.

Time Running Out was photographed by Eugene Shuftan, one of Europe's finest cameramen. Nearly seventy, Gene was more agile and active than any of us. An international linguist, he would frequently address his French colleagues in English, his director in German, and Dane Clark in French. A wonderful man and a wonderful artist.

In the 1948–1949 period when we shot *Time Running Out*, the French technical equipment was inferior to the Hollywood brand. For example, the French camera operator worked without a finder. He looked through a tiny aperture which showed the action through the film itself. I tried peering at the actors and all I could see were blurred shadows, yet apparently practice makes perfect because the results are faultless, even when it came to following a fast-moving car. However, our skillful operator did develop a one-eyed squint during the shooting. The French did have an excellent process screen and equipment, but some of the Hollywood adjuncts were lacking. For instance, the American grips have a revolving thingamy which throws moving shadows on the faces of the actors in a traveling car. In Paris this effect was obtained by the grips, electricians, and prop men carrying branches and circling a light to throw the shadows. The French have an impish humor which is very much like ours. Our process shots were silent, so, as they moved around the light, they all began to dance and sing, swishing the whole performance. It was all I could do to watch the scene. The off-stage ballet was vastly more entertaining.

The French are enormously inventive and ingenious. If something is lacking, they whip up a substitute. Our prop man, "Petit Raymond," was a wizard and a born comic. Between takes he would get Dane Clark in a corner and pantomime risqué stories. In the scene where Michel André's cat reacts to the gas fumes and leaps close to Michel's face, we had rigged up an enclosure around them so that the cat couldn't escape. We also had an invisible piece of glass between Michel and the cat so that it wouldn't actually scratch the actor. We did that later in a big close-up of André with a false paw. Now came a real problem. Monsieur Cat sat comfortably on the stove and wouldn't budge. Petit Raymond yelled at him, offered him catnip from off scene—every lure and threat he could think of. Nothing. Finally, Raymond stood close behind the obstinate feline and fired a forty-five. The cat took off like Tom Sawyer's did when he fed it the Pain Killer.

In addition to being a first-rate actor, Michel André was a wonderful sport. He was slugged, scratched, and kicked, and took it all with a grin. We finally presented him with a grateful memento. Dane Clark made a speech which Simone translated for the benefit of the assembled company. It was a real entente cordiale.

One final, sad postscript. A hassle between Pahlen and Gordine—what it was all about I never fully understood—resulted in our picture being released only in Europe. To this day, Henry Kane—who sent me a flock of wonderful, unprintable letters while I was in Paris, has never seen what he wrote. Too bad. It was a good one.

Before Dane Clark returned to the U.S., he arranged for me to sign up with his agent, one of the all-powerful Hollywood behemoths with a Paris branch. He arranged for a job in Vienna where an American director had been taken ill and returned to Hollywood.

CHAPTER 22

In a few days I was on my way to Austria. The story, *The Magic Face*, was about an impersonator whose wife becomes enamored of Adolph Hitler and ends up as his mistress. The impersonator works out an elaborate scheme to become the assistant to the director's valet and kill the Führer.

In Vienna I stayed at an American press club where a number of our foreign correspondents were living, as well as several members of our state department. In discussing the picture with them before we began to photograph it, I discovered that they felt there was a serious political danger in the concluding episodes. As the script was written, the impersonator's plot succeeds and he takes Hitler's place, purposely making decisions which eventually lose the war and end Hitler's power. The state department people feared that such a conclusion would imply that if the real Hitler had lived his "genius" would have conquered the world. They had pointed this out to the American producer, but he thought they were needlessly concerned and refused to change the plot. Luther Adler was to play both the impersonator and the real Hitler. He and I were worried that their fears might be justified. Since the picture would begin and end with a narration, I suggested that the touchy point could be avoided if the narrator explained that our story was one of the innumerable fantasies that were still going the rounds in Germany and Austria to alibi Hitler's defeat. Our producer was unconvinced. He still thought that we and the state department men were making a mountain out of a molehill. So that was that.

The Adler family has been an outstanding one in the American theatre for many years. Luther and his sister, Stella, have both contributed many notable performances which have added to the luster of the plays they have appeared in and the Adler name. Luther's approach to playing the role of Adolph Hitler was original and highly successful. He ran reel after reel of news shots of the Führer, and deduced the inner character of the man from his outer mannerisms. Patricia Knight played the Eva Braun-like woman who deserts her husband for Hitler. For the most part, the rest of the cast was made up of English-speaking Austrian actors. Peter Preisis, an Austrian-born American actor, played a jail warden, and also coached the Austrians whose English needed polishing. There were three wonderful theatres in Vienna during our stay there. Among those playing in these state-controlled institutions were Curt Jurgens and O.V. Fischer. I had the privilege of watching them both in some truly magnificent productions. Among the actresses we used was the talented Ilka Windisch, then the wife of Joe Israels, an American correspondent who handled our publicity and was a fine and helpful friend. We were able to use a series of spacious real interiors, which were large enough to hold our studio lights. Our Swiss cameraman, Braun, did a great job photographing these interiors, and did equally well in the studio and the streets of Vienna.

During our stay in this once gay city on the blue Danube—which is a muddy yellow—Vienna was under the alternating command of the English, the Russians, and the Americans. Most of the Viennese seemed to be dreaming of the good old days of Strauss, and appeared to be living almost totally in the past. The present, except for the theatre, seemed to be sadly lacking in new creative talents in music and the other arts. The general atmosphere of this once waltzing city was pervaded with melancholy.

Shortly before his death, Felix Basch, famous in Vienna both as a director and actor previous to his coming to the United States, had played one of the hostages in the picture of that name which I've already told you about. I had renewed my friendship with Felix's widow, Greta Basch, just before I sailed for Europe at a studio party given by her son, Peter, the talented portrait photographer. Just after I'd finished shooting *The Magic Face*, Greta and I met again in Vienna. She was on her way to Remagen, Germany, to supervise the dubbing of several European films into English. I knew nothing about this important corollary to motion pictures, so when Greta asked me if I'd be interested in trying my hand at it, the chance to learn something about the trick from experts sounded intriguing enough for me to say yes.

In Remagen, a German concern, the International Film Union, was and still is, the best equipped and most experienced outfit in this complicated business. Remagen on the Rhine, which is less than a half hour from Bonn, is the tiny town where the bridge was blown up during the Allied invasion. Greta's assistant, Robert Myerson, had stage-managed a number of Broadway shows, and was an extremely capable and likeable young American. We went right to work learning the new technique. I'll explain some of its elements.

First of all, the print of the picture to be dubbed is split up into small segments of three or four speeches, and we were supplied with a literal translation. Next, we started running the first little piece over and over and over. As you can imagine, the trick of writing dialogue which will not only match the lip movements of the foreign actors but also sound like American talk, takes a great deal of ingenuity. Bob Myerson caught on much more quickly than I did. As a matter of fact, I never got to be as good as he, but I finally did learn the job.

The most important problem you have to wrestle with is the labials in the original language. These are the letters, which make the speaker close his lips—B, P, M, and to a certain degree F, PH, V, and the WH sound in words like *what* and *where*. If you'll stand in front of a mirror and speak a few sentences containing these letters, you'll see how your lips come together and that, as far as the movement of the lips is concerned, you can substitute an M for a B or a WH for an F and the spectator will be none the wiser. You also keep your eye on open sounds like O which affect the lips of the speaker. Otherwise, believe it or not, you can substitute pretty much any syllable you like for another. But you have to be careful. For example, you can't use "the watch on the Rhine" for "Die Wacht am Rhine" because of the M in the German word "am." However, you could probably get away with "the watch upon the Rhine" if the actor could time his reading to take care of the extra syllable in "upon" and the short word "the" before Rhine, which wouldn't be too tough. The rhythm of the original speech is also important. The English-speaking actor must follow the lilt of the original.

When Bob and I had finished writing the speeches for the first picture we dubbed, we tried them out on one of the English-speaking local experts. He found only a few imperfect spots. We corrected these errors and that part of the job was done. The next job was casting English-speaking actors. At this Greta Basch was indefatigable. There were a number of professionals in the ranks of the American army stationed in Germany. Greta found the actresses in a nearby development, which was jokingly referred to as Westchester on the Rhine—a beautiful community built after the war quite close to Remagen. The actresses, most of whom were the wives of state department officials, donated their salaries to a charity, but the army was able to cooperate by giving the soldier-actors leaves of absences and okaying their paychecks. One of the available actresses was Helen Taylor Munro, the wife of an attorney who was working for the government. She had acted professionally in the United States and in England. Her close friend, Tina Carver, was another tried-and-true pro, but unhappily for us—though happily for her—she was about to give birth to a daughter at the time we needed her. But the most extraordinary discovery we made was sixteen-year-old Karla Most, the daughter of government official, Amicus Most. Helen Munro was present when Karla read for Bob and me. It was a difficult, emotional scene. Helen's eyes widened. "This girl is fantastic," she said later. "Practically no experience and she reads like an old trouper!" I need hardly add that Karla and Helen became fast friends.

Greta assigned me to direct the actual dubbing. To do this, a short piece of the original film is run for the actors who face a mike and a music stand which holds their dialogue. The foreign language sound is then turned off and the actors read their lines, watching the lip movements on the screen. When they feel comfortable with the performance and the director has okayed the feeling of the reading, a take is made. One of the German experts notes where anyone's speed is "out of sync," explains how the tempo can be corrected, and we try it again. Usually we got a perfect reading and perfect lip matching by the third or fourth take. During the dubbing sessions Bob Myerson and I both acted a character or two, and we both discovered what a fiendishly difficult job it is.

When we finally finished the dubbing chore at Remagen, I took off for Italy. Before I left, I talked with a number of Germans and Austrians who had lived under Hitler. They all claimed to have been unaware of the tortures and wholesale murders their leader had been responsible for. Finally I met one German woman who was much more frank. She explained that Hitler had played upon the German psychology by assuring his people that the Versailles Treaty had made them despised and spat upon, when they should and could be the greatest people on Earth.

The victories of the armies of the Third Reich gave their egos a terrific lift, and made it easy to believe the big lies they were told. To be the conquerors of the world seemed to be their destiny and worth any sacrificed to attain. When defeat came and the idea that they were a Master

Race suddenly exploded, they were in despair. In this woman's city, American occupation troops took over. She had expected to be relocated once more to the role of someone beneath contempt; but before long she, and the rest of the Germans, discovered that most of these open-faced youngsters were a bunch of naïve but friendly guys. Then came an extraordinary experience. The American officer for whom she worked seemed to be totally lacking in any urge for revenge. He treated her and the rest of her countrymen with consideration, and, in addition, she found him extremely attractive. Then she discovered that he was a Jew. This revelation turned everything she had been taught to believe topsy-turvy. She began to question him—to try to dig out the truth. His answers were full of understanding and not at all didactic. When I met her, she was very clear about the hideous humbug she and the rest of the German people had swallowed. Her mind was no longer obsessed with dreams of superior and inferior beings, nor was it sick with guilt. She was a healthy-minded human being.

CHAPTER 23

After a brief stay in Italy, I decided to brave the uncertainties of Hollywood despite the slump, which had hit the film capital according to the American picture people I ran across on the Via Veneto. Apparently the tremendous success of television, with its free presentation of Westerns, private-eye mysteries, and sports newscasts, had made a big dent in picture making except for a few super-dupers made at the big studios. I felt that, as someone had rephrased the old maxim, absence makes the heart grow fonder—of someone near at hand. Certainly if you stay away too long, producers are likely to dismiss your name when it comes up by saying, "Oh, he's in Europe." So I flew back.

En route I did a lot of thinking about my profession. Aside from being concerned with getting started again, I had had plenty of time to consider the changes which had taken place in the industry. I began to wonder if I'd been too busy making moving pictures to have analyzed seriously exactly what they are.

Some excellent books have been written about practically every aspect of cinematics. The one I recalled most vividly was Lewis Jacobs' *The Rise of the American Film*. Jacobs had started with the earliest movies at the end of the nineteenth century, when the astonishing fact that they moved had been enough to attract a considerable audience to the nickelodeons.

Georges Melies, a French caricaturist and magician, and been the originator of storytelling with a series of "artificially arranged scenes." He had accented trick effects. Later, in the early 1900s, Edwin S. Porter had been the real father of the story film. His *The Great Train Robbery* was a tremendous success. Although David Wark Griffith is credited with inventing the close-up, Porter did have one very close shot at the end of his picture. The bandit chief fired his revolver directly into the camera. But, with this exception, Porter shot all the rest of his film in full shots. Apparently, he used his close-up only as a shocker—a stunt.

I remembered something else in Jacobs' book which had surprised me. Some of the early films had a message—a point of view, frequently that of the average American beset by the problems of making a living. However, this approach continually changed, where it existed at all, and became more or less anti-social and Pollyanna-like until the time of Woodrow Wilson. I mention this because I had always thought that pictures with ideas were practically non-existent until talkies made discussion possible. For the most part, certainly, movies told their stories in terms of action. Good triumphed and evil was defeated.

Improvements in photography, in the film itself, and in the style of acting marked the growth of the new medium, and that is still true today. Jacobs' book, which I recommend to anyone who is seriously interested in the moving picture, credits one man in particular and three foreign sources as the main contributors to the advance of the quality in this new entertainment and art form. The man was David Wark Griffith, the first director to use inter-cutting to intensify suspense and, in addition to numberless other innovations, this leading American filmmaker fully utilized the vast scope which had originally been used by the Italians in pictures like *Quo Vadis?* and *Cabiria*. These imported canvasses with their gigantic scenic vistas were the first foreign element to influence American picture making. The second came from Germany and featured strange angles and moving camera shots. The third importation came from Russia. The Soviet filmmakers were the first deliberately to use the moving picture to educate and propagandize the viewer—to implant ideas in his mind. The Russians also introduced montage—a series of quick, short cuts of fades and inanimate objects.

With the coming of sound, Mr. Jacobs describes the many innovations which changed the whole approach to picture making, not only in the field of recording, but, indirectly, in many other aspects of the film industry. Naturally there have been other changes after the period where Jacobs' book ends. Momentary popularity was achieved by the introduction of third-dimension devices, but only *Cinerama* has survived, doubtless because the other inventions necessitated the audience wearing special eyeglasses. We have also seen a change in the shape of the screen, accenting the horizontal. This novelty has been effective for mass movement, but when the camera is close there are frequently vast empty spaces on either side of the actor.

Lewis Jacobs pays a high and deserved tribute to Walt Disney, whom he describes as a modern Aesop—a teller of fables. His cartoons are all stamped with an approach which is strikingly his own, and which reflect the violence of the real world which surrounds his fantasies. Today Walt Disney is unquestionably the outstanding creator in the moving picture world. His films are serious, funny, poetic, and tragic. And he never stops experimenting. An interesting sidelight on one phase of his contribution to the movies is the fact that his triumphant use of slapstick practically ended the career of the former mastermind in this field, Mack Sennett.

Naturally my resumé of Jacobs' book and the latest happenings in the world of motion pictures wasn't half so orderly as what I've just written. Many other thoughts rattled around in my head as I flew back home; but finally I did begin to ask myself what was the essence of the movies—what makes them unique? What was it, I wondered, that had survived the continual changes and made their drawing power different from all other forms of entertainment? The more I thought about this, the more I became convinced that the answer was much too complex to be stated arbitrarily and finally. It seemed to me that the best approach to the query was to suggest a possible answer and hope that the wise and creative people who contribute to picture making today would at least agree that the question deserves more serious pondering than has heretofore been given it.

I imagine that everyone will agree that telling a story with a camera, a microphone, and actors is the basic essential common to most motion pictures; but I believe it is also true that the creative minds behind the process must constantly remind themselves that moving pictures will remain unique only if their particular potential is realized to the utmost. They must also be conscious that the medium is different from a novel, a play, or a treatise. Basically it must always be a picture which moves, not only in terms of action, but in terms of feeling. If this concept is kept in mind, ideas may be discussed, emotions may be aroused, and joy and laughter and hope may be evoked. Obviously this brief analysis is only the buzzing of a gadfly. All I am trying to say to picture makers is, "Think about it!" The rest is silence.

Milton Bren gave me my first job when I returned to Hollywood after a five-year absence. He had been working on the script of a Western with a young writer, Blake Edwards, but this talented scenarist was on the

Frank Tuttle and Alan Ladd.

point of leaving to fulfill a previous commitment. A few years after this Blake created the stories for the TV series, *Peter Gunn*, several of which he directed. He has also directed a number of feature pictures. To paraphrase what Emile Couée said some years ago, "Day by day, in every way, Blake is getting better and better." As I've already mentioned, Milton Bren's wife is Claire Trevor. Aside from being a brilliant actress, Claire is an excellent painter. It was a heart-warming experience to be welcomed home by two such delightful friends.

While I was completing the screenplay with Milton, I renewed my friendship with Sue and Alan Ladd. Through their efforts I was assigned by Warner Brothers to direct Alan's next picture, *Hell on Frisco Bay*, which co-starred Edward G. Robinson, with whom I'd never had the pleasure of working.

The screenplay had been started by a fine writer, Sydney Boehm, but, as had been the case with Blake Edwards, he too had to fulfill another assignment, and the script was finished by Martin Rackin, who is now one of the top executives at Paramount. Marty was a good friend of Sydney, so the collaboration was mutually agreeable. In addition to his talents, Marty Rackin is a wit and a delightful raconteur. His presence during the shooting in San Francisco was a big boost to our morale.

Hell on Frisco Bay told the story of a San Francisco police detective, played by Alan Ladd, who is being released from San Quentin, where he had done time for supposedly being involved in a police scandal. The frame-up had been cleverly planned by Amato, the ruthless head of a labor organization, played by Edward G. Robinson. To prevent his wife being hounded by Amato's henchmen, Alan had refused to contact her during his prison term. Feeling that she had been rejected and hurt by her husband's apparent indifference, the wife—Joanne Dru—has had a brief affair with a musician in the orchestra with which she appears as the singing soloist. The prison grapevine had gotten word of this to Alan and had added to the bitterness already engendered by the unjust conviction. His return to freedom finds him obsessed with only one purpose, to revenge himself on Amato and his corrupt associates.

But he must also clear himself. He has only one ally, his detective sidekick, played by William Demarest. Bit by bit, they begin to piece together the complex elements of the frame-up. Amato's organization includes a gunman with a scarred face whose girl was once a picture actress. These roles were played by Paul Stewart and Fay Wray. Amato's wife is a deeply religious woman who dotes on Amato's nephew, a young punk who is more interested in girls than in his uncle's corrupt business and its complex ramifications.

Among the characters Alan visits is an honest labor leader—Nestor Paiva—whose disgust at Amato's ruthless rise to power has driven him to console himself with the bottle. From this man and others Alan slowly begins to assemble the hidden evidence. Simultaneously William Demarest continues trying to bring Alan and his wife together. Alan finally roughs up Amato's nephew and makes him spill enough facts to make Amato feel the youngster talks too much. He has the boy killed. Shortly after this Amato decides to get out of town and flee the country. When his gunman, Paul Stewart, tries to stop him, Amato kills him and starts for the wharfs. En route he seizes Joanne Dru as a hostage. Alan catches up with him in time to free Joanne, but Amato escapes in a motorboat. Alan dives from the pier and grabs the boat's gunwale before it picks up speed. He clambers aboard and the two men fight as the motorboat speeds across San Francisco Bay with no one at the wheel—narrowly missing several huge oncoming craft. William Demarest commandeers a police launch and pursues the struggling men, who dive overboard just before Amato's motorboat crashes into the concrete base which supports the San Francisco Bridge. The police launch picks them up. Amato is jailed and Alan and Joanne are reunited.

Directing an Alan Ladd picture was an ideal way to re-establish myself. Alan always surrounds himself with superb actors. Edward G. is a master performer and a great guy. Between shots, he loves to clown around. Just before the start of the motorboat chase, the blanks in his automatic didn't go off. He immediately put on a terrific act. In a strange accent he screamed that this was the first time in his career that a Warner Brothers gun had failed him. As we howled encouragement, he beat his breast and wept. Let me use the fine performances in *Hell on Frisco Bay* as an excuse to say a word or two about moving picture acting.

CHAPTER 24

"Speak the speech, I pray you, as I pronounced it to you, trippingly on the tongue but if you mouth it, as many of your players do, I had as lief the town-crier spoke my lines. Nor do not saw the air too much with your hand, thus; but use all gently: for in the very torrent, tempest, and as I may say the whirlwind of passion, you must acquire and beget a temperance, that may give it smoothness. Oh, it offends me to the soul to hear a robustious periwig-pated fellow tear a passion to tatters, to very rags, to split the ears of the groundlings, who for the most part are capable of nothing but inexplicable dumb-shows and noise. I would have such a fellow whipped for o'erdoing termagant; it out-herod's Herod...Suit the action to the word, the word to the action; with this special observance, that you o'erstep not the modesty of nature...

"To hold, as 'twere, the mirror up to nature; to show virtue her own feature, scorn her own image, and the very age and body of the time his form and pressure...I have thought some of nature's journeyman had made men and not made them well, they imitated humanity so abominably..."

These quotations are, of course, excerpts from Hamlet's speech to the players.

We sometimes forget that Shakespeare was an actor as well as a playwright and poet. In any case, Hamlet's advice is still valid, I believe, although more than three hundred years have elapsed since Burbage first delivered the speech at the Globe Theatre.

But if Shakespeare's advice continues to be sound, acting and the theatre have changed in many respects since then. The plays of Henrik Ibsen, filled with social comment in addition to their compelling dramatic structure, started a whole new trend in their day. After Ibsen, even plays with nothing to say were forced to give a surface illusion of reality;

and in the realm of acting, performers found that Shakespeare's mirror held up to nature had taken on a new significance with the changing times. To satisfy their new audiences, actors found they must dig deeper and deeper into the depths of the characters they were portraying. This accent on realism culminated in the work of the Moscow Art Theatre actors, directed by Constantine Stanislavski. All over the world the acting profession was stimulated to watch the fine results of his Method.

Today a reaction has set in. Method acting is ridiculed in some quarters, largely, it seems to me, because a few of its advocates went in for mumbling in a tee-shirt; but Stanislavski's insistence that an actor should know the roots and background of the character he is playing is difficult to refute. *An Actor Prepares* will give anyone who is interested in the subject an excellent summary of how Stanislavski worked. My friends used to kid me for saying, "Believe it!" just before a take started. What I was trying to do, of course, was to remind the players to think who they were and concentrate on the situation in which they found themselves. I believe a performance involves a willful preparation in addition to the talent the actor has fallen heir to.

In a recent article in *Esquire*, critic Dwight MacDonald agrees with the late James Agee that "few Americans either behind or in front of our cameras give any recognition or respect for themselves or one another as human beings. . . . I suppose it will some day be possible to deduce that the supposedly strongest nation on Earth collapsed with such magical speed because so few of its members honored any others, or even themselves, as human beings." MacDonald goes on to say that "in foreign films, one often gets individuals . . . but in even the most 'serious' Hollywood films, one gets stereotypes." To quote him again, he further declares that "developing an acting style is not the same thing as exploiting mannerisms," and he criticizes American actors for starting with striking individual performances and ending up with constant repetitions of the original performance.

This is a harsh criticism, but although there is some truth in it, I believe the result he decries is more universal than American, and that its cause is largely due to the necessity of films making money. This situation exists to a greater or lesser degree everywhere in the world except in Soviet Russia, and there the accent on propaganda is so pronounced that today the Russian films, with few exceptions, display even less individual human beings than ours do.

It seems to me that any analysis of what is behind the small percentage of great pictures and performances must start with the realization that a great film is enormously difficult to achieve; and because moving pictures is an industry which aims at profit as well as quality, the producing company must produce what are considered commercial films in sufficient quantity to balance the output of the unusual and the daring, or the producing company will collapse.

Apropos of this, I recently finished reading the autobiography of the distinguished director, King Vidor, which was published something over a year ago, and I noted that he shares my feeling about the necessity of making profitable motion pictures and its result. He says, "When a producer spends a couple of million dollars, he is inclined to stick to the tried-and-true formulas to assure the return of his money, so that high production costs have a tendency to stifle originality and experimentation."

It is also true that a considerable number of American filmmakers are constantly trying to achieve something as close to greatness as their combined talents can create. The chances of accomplishing this in the field of popular entertainment are bound to be limited no matter how hard the creators try. Even if we assume that those with integrity are trying to find material and personnel to produce outstanding pictures, they must also fill in with the best stories and craftsmen available to stay alive. This is particularly true of the individuals involved. For example, an actor like Ernest Borgnine had to play dozens of conventional heavies before *Marty* came along, and even after his performance brought him recognition, he had to go on acting in other roles, less challenging and less satisfying to him as an artist. The chance of finding all the elements necessary to achieve greatness is rare. And, I believe, in the kind of world we live in, that will always be true. Mr. MacDonald is quite right to holler. His hollering helps. But the great pictures and the great performances he is yelling about are one hell of a tough reality to achieve. About that I'm certain.

Many viewers feel that moving pictures accent personalities rather than talent. Ideally, of course, the perfect picture actor should have both these attributes. I believe that a thoughtful appraisal of acting in the theatre will disclose that personality has always been a big drawing card there, even before there were any movies. Audiences have always taken personalities to their hearts; but it is also true that most of the actors and actresses born with this special appeal, to their credit be it said, have worked hard to become better actors.

People outside the world of pictures and theatre are often curious to know if there is any real difference between picture acting and stage acting. In both mediums, I believe, the essentials are the same; but the presence of the camera did change the actor's approach considerably. Thinking photographs, and the closer the camera is the less the actor has to project. Acting without an audience also affects the performance. Picture actors work for the camera and the director. Before he died, that fine gentlemen, actor, and director, Irving Pichel, once pointed out to me that one of the fundamental differences between stage and screen was that a play *is happening*, while a picture *has already happened*, before the audience sees it. Most Hollywood actors have appeared in the theatre, but not all of them. When the movies started talking, many of the stars had never been in a play; but the great majority adapted themselves to the new medium quickly and successfully. As I've already pointed out, the basic qualities that make for good acting are the same in any métier; and every imaginable kind of person may be a good actor. Some of them are particularly creative and bring freshness and life to every character they portray. Others are effective craftsmen who put themselves completely in the hands of the director; and there are all sorts of variations between those two. One thing is certain. The director should try to inspire the full potential of the players he works with. I like most actors, and I'm happy they are willing to accept me as their audience.

With the exception of the news and other actual happenings which are photographed, the production of television is the production of short moving pictures with a somewhat limited scope because the TV screen is small. Live TV, of course, is a kind of short play which is being photographed while it is happening. If the quality of most television is inferior to that of the best movies, we must consider how much younger it is, and must also realize that its viewers are a mass audience which selects from what is available by twisting a dial, and without going to the trouble and expense which causes the picturegoer to make a more thoughtful choice.

The average half-hour TV show is shot in three days and sometimes with no preliminary rehearsals. All the departments involved do a terrific job of preparation, which is a lifesaver for the director because he must move at top speed the minute the shooting begins. For him to get the kind of unusual camera angles which have made the *Peter Gunn* series outstanding in this respect takes great ingenuity. Blake Edwards told me that he, the cameraman and the rest of the technical crew, plan every shot in advance. During the shooting there just isn't time to work out odd angles. Working at top speed is a challenge, but for three days, it is not too difficult to maintain this pace without the quality suffering if you take the time to prepare. Everyone knows what's next, and everyone—actors, cameramen, and the crew—really moves.

My first job in television was one of the anti-communist series, *Crusader*, starring Brian Keith, an accomplished and highly intelligent actor. Following this I directed two TV shows starring Alan Ladd, and one of the Directors' Guild series, "Claire," which starred George Montgomery and Angela Lansbury. For an old-timer like me, directing TV was exciting. I got a real kick out of the challenge of making them both fast and good.

No matter how quickly TV dramas develop and mature, one point is obvious. In the field of reality, television is unique. The outcome of a sporting event has a suspense that even the greatest fiction can't possibly compete with because no one knows who's going to win—unless it's been fixed of course. News events are greatly enhanced by that emotionless monster, the camera, which has an eye but no heart. The quality of the figures in the happenings of today stands naked before the world. How lucky we were to have seen and heard Mr. Kennedy versus Mr. Nixon. What a pity that the Lincoln-Douglas debates were not photographed and recorded. This TV service we have is certainly unique and invaluable.

CHAPTER 25

There is some kind of an income tax or capital gains gimmick which makes it obligatory for a picture star with his own company to produce a certain number of films in which he doesn't appear himself. This obligation was one of the reasons for Alan Ladd's Jaguar Company producing *A Cry in the Night* at Warner Brothers. I was happy that Alan selected me as its director because it was a good story with an excellent screenplay by David Dortort, and a group of fine actors. Among them were Natalie Wood, Edmond O'Brien, Raymond Burr, Brian Donlevy, Irene Hervey, Peter Hanson, Richard Anderson, and Tina Carver, the actress I'd met in Germany.

David Dortort had given the original story an interesting psychiatric background. A possessive mother has monopolized her grown son to a point where he has practically no life of his own except for dreams which are never fulfilled. This strange character, played by Raymond Burr, has wandered to the local Lovers' Lane to watch with envy the goings on in the parked cars. It so happens that a police detective's daughter (Natalie Wood) has driven to this spot with her boyfriend (Richard Anderson) to discuss their plans for getting married. Their choosing this particular secret place is the result of her father's experience with reprehensible characters having made him super protective. His over-strictness with his daughter has led his wife to beg the police detective (Edmond O'Brien) to be more lenient, but he has insisted that Natalie is still a child.

When the young man discovers Burr snooping in the underbrush, he jumps out of the car and confronts the psycho. When he gets tough, Burr slugs him with his lunch box; then, fearful that Anderson may be dead, Burr grabs the girl and drives off with her.

When Anderson comes to, he is apprehended as a possible drunk by the occupants of a police car. At the police station, Edmond O'Brien's superior officer played by Brian Donlevy, questions the boy and learns that the abducted girl is O'Brien's daughter. With Anderson in tow, he goes to his fellow officer's house.

Meanwhile Burr has driven the girl to an abandoned factory in downtown Los Angeles, where he has a hideout. When she pleads with him to release her, he is still afraid that the boy may be dead. He begins to talk about himself and his mother, his sex-starved eyes constantly on the girl's appealing face and figure.

When O'Brien learns what has happened, he swears he will kill the abductor if he finds him. Brian Donlevy reminds him that he is in charge of the case and declares that he will permit O'Brien to come along only if he promises to accept his orders. Donlevy and Irene Hervey (as Natalie's mother) point out that O'Brien's strictness was partly responsible for Anderson's having been forced to meet Natalie clandestinely. The three men leave Irene Hervey with O'Brien's sister and begin their search for the kidnapped girl.

The gradual narrowing down of the possible places where Burr may have taken the girl finally begin to result in their closing in on Burr's hideout, where Natalie's pretended interest in her captor's past has thus far kept him at a safe distance. The story's climax comes when the pursuers drive into the grounds surrounding the ruins of the abandoned factory.

When they finally close in on the psychopath and his prisoner, the boyfriend of the police detective's daughter saves O'Brien's life by leaping down upon the armed man from a story-high girder and knocking the gun out of his hand. O'Brien takes Natalie in his arms and gruffly includes Anderson in a gesture as he tells him to come home with them. Despite its being a low budget picture, *A Cry in the Night* was a box office winner.

Aside from talking about some of the tricks of my profession, I've said very little about directing motion pictures. When you ponder the various facets of the job you've devoted most of your life to, it is inevitable, I imagine, that you hesitate before setting down your thoughts on paper; but one idea did occur to me that I acted upon immediately. I decided to ask a number of my colleagues to send me their credos concerning the function of the director, and also to tell me what picture they had most enjoyed making. Some of those I wrote to are abroad or haven't answered me for other reasons. The answers I did get I've arranged alphabetically. I hope you'll enjoy reading what they have to say as much as I did.

When Frank Capra was directing for Columbia Pictures, an article in *Vanity Fair* referred to him as the gem of Columbia's ocean. Well said-

and true. Today he is the gem of the Screen Directors' Guild, its president, an office which he previously held during that organization's struggle for recognition.

If you asked a typical moviegoer to name ten directors I believe he'd find it difficult, although our Guild has more than two thousand members. Audiences remember the names of actors, but with a few exceptions, they pay little attention to the name of the man behind the camera. An outstanding exception is Frank Capra. His name is known everywhere. Last summer an article appeared in the *Los Angeles Times* which stated Frank's point of view admirably. I shall quote it here in its entirety.

So you want to be a director?

THINK OF FANS, NOT SELF—FRANK CAPRA

By Marylou Luther

When Frank Capra is making movies, the good guys always win.

In defense of the happy-ending he offers this charge to tomorrow's cinema superintendent: "With a captive audience for two-hour stretches, the director can influence public thinking for good or evil. The responsible one is normally obligated to emphasize the positive qualities of humanity by showing the triumph of the individual over adversities.

"His movies should be a positive impression that there is hope, mercy, justice, and charity. These are the only things of substance, the riches of life."

So-called realistic films of violence and brutality can't be real, he said, if they don't show these positive qualities.

(Capra's evidence of the power of positive pictures: Academy Awards for *It Happened One Night*, *Mr. Deeds Goes to Town*, and *You Can't Take it with You*.)

The positive picture-maker is, to Capra, the one who has mastered his tools. "He must be well-versed in sound, music, the use of the cameras, the editing of film. With these tools, he must be able to tell a tale with imagination and interest. His main job is entertaining the public."

According to the immigrant boy from Italy who won his Oscars by glorifying "the American way," there is no defined route to the top, no prescribed preparation.

"I don't advise following my pre-Hollywood footsteps," grinned the electrical engineer from Caltech.

"It would be helpful if the director were a writer first," he continued, "because fundamentally he's a storyteller. He should be a good audience. He should know and want to know more about people, and he should like them."

Explaining that both UCLA and SC have film courses, including a class in directing, Capra said it really doesn't matter what "school" the director attends—the film editor's, the script writer's, even the actor's—as long as it isn't the school where acting is apparent as acting.

"No one is precluded from directing if he's learned his crafts. Beyond this, it's a matter of perseverance, luck, and opportunity. With everything going for him, the top director can make two or three hundred thousand (dollars) a year.

Capra's big break? "I was born."

Reel one of his advice to the fledgling director opens: "Read a lot, especially screenplays, because they're in dialogue form, and in movies everything must be told in dialogue. The plot and character are revealed through what is said, not through what is thought."

Reel two of the Capra documentary: "Go to the movies." See a picture once for entertainment, he recommends, and then again to find what the director did, how he composed his scenes, what sequences he used to obtain a certain effect, how his tale was constructed.

"There are all kinds of directors," Capra mused, describing "his" type as "the one whose greatest contribution is giving the actors a complete understanding of the character." This is achieved, he pointed out, by discussing the character—"who he is, why he is, what makes him tick, what he wants, and what his dreams are.

"There's no such thing as a bad actor, only bad directors."

John Cromwell, another former president of The Screen Directors' Guild, was a Broadway actor and director before he came to Hollywood. Now living in Connecticut, John gave me a brief but excellent answer to my questions. Here's what he said.

> Dear Frank:
> What a surprise after all these years! My contribution would be as follows.
>
> The director is essentially the teller of the story or shall we say the story weaver. He takes all the elements of the tale and weaves them into a pattern.
>
> *Anna and the King of Siam*, I think, was my happiest experience. Best of luck with your book, Frank.

CHAPTER 26

George Cukor was a noted director in the theatre before he came to Hollywood. He is the particular favorite of many great ladies of the stage and screen, but is equally adept at directing actors. A high grade of intelligence, a dry wit, and a great fund of information on many subjects are among the assets which have made him so successful. The letter accompanying his comments on direction said:

> Dear Frank:
> I'm sorry I was so long getting this to you but I've been away. I hope you can use it. As I reread what I've written I was embarrassed. I made the directors out to be very accomplished people indeed. Well, they are, poor things.
> Kindest regards
> George Cukor

And here is his appraisal of the director's function.

> You ask what picture I most enjoyed making. There's no special one. In some cases, I had a wonderful time directing a picture but the results were far from happy. Other times, it's been a painful business and the picture turned out pretty well. I enjoy working on the picture I'm making, and I look forward with excitement to the next one.
> As for a director's function, that's a tough question to answer. It means trying to put into a nutshell what has taken practically a lifetime to learn—and unlearn. But I'll

try. The director is, first of all, the catalyst—he gets things going. He influences the writing of the script, the casting, the sets, the costumes. When the actual shooting begins he's confronted with actors and a text, and he must make it come to life. With an inexperienced actor, he must be a kind of coach and a teacher. With experienced actors he should be a perceptive and sensitive guide. At all times he should create a sympathetic climate in which the actors and others concerned can function. He's a combination of father confessor and pal, or at least that's what he should try to be. He cannot be all sweetness and light, he'd better have something of the lion tamer in him. All this, and serve as an audience as well. It is his reaction and response that keeps the excitement alive.

As I re-read these letters, I am momentarily prouder and prouder that I belong to the director's profession. How right George Cukor is—a group of very accomplished people. Amen!

Delmer Daves fulfills Frank Capra's advice to add writing to your equipment if you hope to direct. He was a distinguished screenwriter. Here's what he wrote me.

> Dear Frank:
>
> I have just returned from a location hunt and your earlier letter caught me on my return from a brief vacation in La Jolla, after returning from Connecticut—so you can see I have been on the run. Please forgive the delay in answering your request. As to the film I most enjoyed directing, the answer is difficult indeed, for I have had genuine and deep pleasure in doing most of them—only a few were in the "obligation to the studio" category, things I had to do without much alternative, since I was being paid every week and was expected to do something for it! It is interesting and not surprising that these are the films I think the least of and had the least joy in making.
>
> For various reasons, I deeply enjoyed making the following films the most, I believe: *Destination Tokyo* (my first child, so to speak, thus loved as a parent loves a first-born,

for it was my first directorial job); *Pride of the Marines* (because it brought to a climax my earlier efforts at "documentary story telling"—utter realism in truth and style); *Dark Passage* (because I was able to, without trickery, use the *camera* as Humphrey Bogart for the first reels of the film and this was exciting); *Broken Arrow*, for reasons discussed later; my Westerns stories: *Jubal, The Last Wagon, Drumbeat, 3:10 to Yuma, Cowboy, The Hanging Tree* because they come out of my heritage as the descendant of pioneers who crossed the plains, on both sides of my family. *A Summer Place,* as a contemporary investigation into moral issues. You see, I have valid reasons for feeling close to all of these films and more, more than I can list here.

But in searching my heart I think *Broken Arrow* affected me the most—the reasons go deeper than the great purpose of the film, even, for they tap my bloodstream and the grandparents I mentioned above who came through the Indian lands in 1854 and in the 1860s—and were treated kindly by them. I have their diaries—and while they had the usual fears and even the usual threats, the personal contacts were more often helpful than hurtful. I was raised on these tales—and when I took my degree at Stanford University, my reward to myself was to spend three months in the Indian country of Northern Arizona, sleeping out every night and wandering every day—and getting to know the Indian people. They responded to a youth alone, and carried on the tradition my grandparents had known: they were my friends. I was even invited by a Hopi to spend the night before the Snake Dance on the roof of his pueblo house, a rare honor—for I saw the pre-dawn ceremonials and the Antelope Dance as well as the famed Snake Dance.

That was in 1926 when northern Arizona and Monument Valley and the Apache reservations were still primitive lands.

Strangely in all the years that passed, until 1949, I never (during my career as a writer) wrote a Western story nor had I, starting as a Director in 1943, been assigned to any remotely resembling a Western. So, when I went to work at 20th Century-Fox and Darryl Zanuck sent for me and asked me to do *Broken Arrow*, I had all the sudden excitement of entering a new-old world—as though I had been waiting all my life for this opportunity.

The reason I loved making *Broken Arrow* is essentially a simple one: the story opened with James Stewart riding across the Apache desert land and his voice said, "What you are about to see really happened. The only change will be that when the Apache speaks, he will speak in our language, *so you may understand him.*" I saw in those words more than communication by voice, an end to the "Me Indian, Ugh! Him go this way!" kind of Indian. I saw an opportunity to show the Indian as I had known him—a man with a sense of honor and dignity and friendship, even of passionate loyalties, sometimes at great cost to themselves. This became the relationship between James Stewart's character and Cochise, the great Apache leader. But it became more than that—the film became the "first adult Western," the critics said. But it became more than *that*, I found, it struck a responsive note for us as Americans, in that suddenly the world saw a film we made that said, "There were good Americans in the West—and bad ones. There were bad Indians out there—BUT there were good ones, too, great ones!" This seems simple now—but it was a great step forward at the time, in trying to understand a native people, even a savage people, and to find in them the same qualities of honor and dignity and heroism that had hitherto been assigned only to the white man. Thus I felt the film was a tribute to the dignity of man—of all men—and that is why I am proud to have been the director of it.

Cordially,
Del

I have never met José Ferrer, but his remarkable skill both as an actor and director made me feel that his opinion would be a fine addition to the ones I had already asked for. He wrote me as follows:

Dear Mr. Tuttle:

Please don't think me rude for not answering your letter much sooner, but I had to go to New York for a week and left your letter behind by mistake, so here goes:

I think of the director as the author's agent twice. First, he represents the author in his relationship with the actor, since he interprets in actor's lingo what the writer had in mind, and helps the actors find ways and means of putting that intention on the stage. Second, he represents the author in his relationship with the audience, in this case in a second-hand way as he himself is not on the stage or the screen, but he does compose the stage or screen picture and help to bring unity of execution to the finished product, even to the extent that he is responsible for the cutting.

Perhaps it is because of my stage background, where the writer is considered all-important, and where his rights are sacrosanct and all-powerful, but I still believe that the man who puts the words and the actions on what was a blank piece of paper is the most important element in any dramatic production, and if the producer or the director make big contributions to a film production, what is said, what is photographed, and how, then whether they get credit for it or not they are to that extent writers, just as an actor who ad-libs a line that is retained in the script is to that extent a writer.

Naturally, the most democratic endeavor in the world is show business, because every star-actor and star-director depends on so many other people and so many other elements for the ability to function, that I think show business is a lesson in humility and it has always puzzled me that anyone who has been in it any length of time can develop and keep a big ego. The point is that so many functions overlap slightly in a play or picture: the writer and actors help to direct, the actor helps to write, the director is certainly very close to being a co-author, and so on.

I feel a little silly writing about directing to you, but I am pleased and flattered that you wished to hear from me and I hope that this to some extent, fills the bill. I happen to be in love with my profession and nothing is more fun than discussing our line of work, so if you want any more from me, for Heaven's sake, don't hesitate to ask for it. Perhaps you want my remarks beamed in a different direction. Anyway, here it is.

I look forward to meeting you some day and having a drink with you. In the meantime, most cordial regards.

José Ferrer

Please forgive the homemade typing.

I believe you'll agree that I'm a lucky guy to be in a profession where my colleagues can do their stuff so brilliantly and write about it so intelligently.

Elia Kazan was a successful actor and director in the New York theatre before he came out here and directed a great number of outstanding motion pictures, which were acclaimed by public and critics alike. Here is his answer to my cry for help.

Dear Frank:

I am glad you are writing about motion picture directors. Perhaps a couple of sentences from me would do.

The one most important thing in directing a motion picture is emotional conviction about the material. If you have this, most everything else will follow. If you don't, you can flounder—albeit very skillfully all over the place.

It is the core within yourself that you have to rely on.

As to what picture I enjoyed the most—I'd say *On the Waterfront*.

Best Regards,
Elia Kazan

Despite the variety of his directorial achievements, I imagine that the warmth and humor Henry Koster brought to the Deanna Durbin pictures will always be especially remembered. I first met him when he was directing one of them and introduced him to "Pa" Rolfe, my Greek teacher at the Hill School. This scholarly gentleman paid a visit to Hollywood just after he had retired, and had got in touch with me. He was a

Durbin fan, so that meeting her and Bobby Koster, as the director is known to his friends, was a big thrill for him. Here is Henry Koster's answer to my query about motion picture directing.

> Dear Frank:
> It was so nice to hear from you and let me wish you the best of luck for your book.
> Your request is difficult to meet. How can I write to an old master like you about directing? But let me try. Let's see if you agree.
> I consider the Alpha and Omega of each picture the story, the screenplay, and the dialogue. When the talents of author and director can be blended in style and craftsmanship, an enjoyable offering will result, but they must blend. A fine director, of course, can fail with a poor story, but a poor director cannot fail completely with a splendid one.
> The picture I enjoyed making most was *Harvey*. There was that great and warm story by Mary Chase; there was her fine dialogue, and then, of course, there was James Stewart. Last, but not least, there was that loveable Josephine Hull who gained an Oscar for her performance.
> Dear Frank, I hope this will do. If not, holler.
>
> Yours,
> Bobby

CHAPTER 27

Ranking high among present-day directors whose pictures have had something to say about the world we live in is Stanley Kramer. It seems to me that he has always approached this story material with the kind of skill which makes the message seem implicit to the characters and the story without any apparent preachment. I also believe that this calls for a remarkable astuteness and sensitivity. He wrote the following:

Dear Frank:

It was very nice of you to ask me to make comment for your book about direction and I have given it some thought.

The big danger is to become all-knowing or patronizing, even in a statement which is based upon a personal experience. Insofar as I am concerned, I think that each film calls for its own positive technique, and perhaps we had been too unwilling to grasp the potential of the medium in destroying some of the established practices.

There is no ceiling to what may be accomplished creatively with sets and lighting and camera, and I think we have just begun to scratch the surface of what is supposedly an established medium with precise approaches.

I think for pure enjoyment, *The Defiant Ones* was the film I enjoyed most in the making.

All the best,
Stanley

Spartacus, Paths of Glory, and *The Killing* are among the outstanding pictures directed by Stanley Kubrick, whom I have never met, but who wrote me from Elstree, England.

> Dear Mr. Tuttle:
> Many thanks for your note about the book, which has just been forwarded to me. I am in the midst of work her and haven't been able to think of anything sensible enough to write that I'd dare see published in a book.
>
> Best Regards,
> Stanley

Another former president of our Guild, George Marshall, has the extraordinary record of having directed 411 feature pictures. While he is particularly adept with comedy, his impressive list of the pictures has included every conceivable type of story. George had this to say in responce to my letter.

> Dear Frank:
> To answer your second question first, I've enjoyed directing all the pictures I've been associated with, but one of them, *Destry Rides Again*, starring Marlene Dietrich and Jimmy Stewart, was a particularly enjoyable experience, because the career of a fine actress and a fine lady had been teetering, and, after *Destry*, Marlene returned to the top spot where she belonged, and has been there ever since. To have contributed to this made me especially happy.
> As far as the director's function is concerned, the facets of the job are so many and so complex, that I can best sum them up, I believe, by saying that he has to be a magician. To develop this idea a bit further, we all discover that sooner or later in addition to being a Jack-of-all-trades, we have to pull that rabbit out of the hat. For example, you may have counted on star X playing the leading role, and be told at the last moment that the powers that be have suddenly handed you Joe Blow—a fine actor, but so

totally different from X that the whole conception of the character and the story has to be quickly revised.

To give a concrete illustration of this magician-like character of the director, in one picture, with hundreds of extras on location miles from anywhere, it became suddenly evident that instead of having one hero, we had two: one the father, the other the son. If we had left the yarn as it was written, we would have inevitably divided our audiences into two rooting sections. I made a quick decision. We had to kill off the father. In another picture, *The Blue Dahlia*, starring Alan Ladd, one of the heavies broke his toe. Too much of the picture had already been shot to substitute another actor. Once again the director had suddenly to make up his mind and pull a Houdini. This time I introduced a new scene which dramatized the injury. We were in business again. From that point on, the actor could limp.

These may sound like a couple of rare instances, but actually, the unexpected happens quite frequently. Yes, the motion picture director must certainly be a magician. Presto! Change-o! Alacazam!

Aside from his also having been a Guild president, George Stevens is unquestionably one of the most distinguished and talented members of his profession. As I write this, he is in the midst of preparing *The Greatest Story Ever Told* with another great American, Carl Sandburg. The titles of just a few of the pictures George has produced and directed read like a list of some of the greatest pictures ever made. *A Place in the Sun, Giant, The Diary of Anne Frank* are among them. It should also be noted that the Stevens touch has also displayed his unique talent for comedy. *The More the Merrier* was an outstanding example of this gift.

George Stevens wrote me as follows:

Dear Frank:

I did enjoy hearing from you and I planned to dash off a reply between chores, but I got stuck for answers. How did you think of two questions that would prove to be such stickers? "A statement about the functions of the motion picture director"—the definition of this I have not as yet resolved in my mind. I find myself from day to day threshing about in an activity that I perhaps hope will, by nature of its own course, eventually present your answer. At this moment, I find myself totally unprepared to presume a definition.

The other high hurdle: "the name of the picture you most enjoyed making." A brief attempt at reflection in this direction turned me to tomorrow, with the hope that the next one will be the one that I enjoy.

I must thank you, Frank, for graciously wishing to include me in your work, and please let me say that I will be very happy to affirm your definitions to the above.

Fraternally,
George

Norman Taurog and a second favorite Norman of mine, Norman McLeod, got their directorial starts as a result of my being in the middle of a job. The picture they were assigned to was a joyful, wacky vehicle with a number of fine comics, among them, Leon Errol. After the two Normans had been working for a week or so, the studio head was upset by a gag they had whipped up for the superb comedian with the rubber legs, and asked me to have a look at it. This was it. Leon Errol approached a small mailbox on a train, but his letter was too large to fit into the opening, so he solemnly tore it in two and inserted the halves. Alone in the projection room, I emitted a loud guffaw, rushed back to the boss, and told him the boys were doing great. I only wished I had thought of the gag. There were no more complaints, and they both went on, together and separately, to directing some of the greatest laugh-getters ever made. Norman Taurog was at Fox when I asked him would he. He did. Here it is.

Dear Frank:

This probably will be much too long, but having edited one or two pictures in your life, I am sure you can cut it down to ten or fifteen reels.

I like to direct motion pictures because: 1) it is a great medium in which to express yourself, especially if you're a frustrated actor; 2) having directed so many young people in my career, it has enabled me to derive great satisfaction in helping to bring out talents that they knew nothing about.

There is no greater thrill than sitting in an audience and hearing the laughter rock a theatre and know that you're a small part in helping to give pleasure and relief from the trials and tribulations in a hectic world.

I also like people; and being a part of this great industry in a directorial way, and handling as many young people as I have in the past and hope to in the future, it keeps you young yourself. Hurrah for Youth!!

Sincerely,
Norman

My favorite pictures: *Skippy, Boys Town, Room for One More.*

King Vidor was not only our Guild's first president and the author of *A Tree is a Tree*, his autobiography, but he is known all over the world as a prominent figure in the motion picture industry. Just the other day the following appeared in Hedda Hopper's column in the *Los Angeles Times*.

VIDOR STRIKES AT VIOLENCE IN FILMS
Director Warns 'Extra Buck' Boys to Regard Danger Signs
By Hedda Hopper

"I don't want to direct pictures filled with violence and gore nor do I want to see them. All over the nation people are protesting the kind of stories we've been making. Mothers of young children say they can't take them to the movies any more. The guy who's in this business to make an extra buck without regard for what is good for the whole had better look out and be sure he's going to have a bank account. What is the date the Commies set to take over? 1972, isn't it?"

It's King Vidor speaking, one of our great directors. He filmed *War and Peace* and *Solomon and Sheba* abroad, has been preparing his next picture, *Conquest*, for a year.

"I've been thinking about it. It's an original about a man who wants to find himself, who and what he really is; a motion picture director doing a big spectacular Biblical film declares he won't do any more like that, something in him revolts at keeping on doing the same old stuff. He goes off to his childhood home, a small town, to recapture the integrity of his youth before he sold out for materialism. Bill Holden or Frank Sinatra could play it. Frank has a kind of genius. I hope he doesn't start trying to direct."

STANDARD OF EXCELLENCE

King Vidor's *Big Parade* set an all-time standard of excellence. There was no Academy then so he didn't get an Oscar, although he's been nominated seven times since. *Hallelujah* was the first all-Negro picture and among the first to be done in documentary style. "It's still running," he said, "So's *The Crowd*. Audrey and Mel Ferrer stood in line on the Left Bank recently to see it."

"Why do you think today's stars are so aggressive about taking over this business?" I asked him.

"Perhaps it has something to do with the tax structure; or maybe they feel they want their own company so they can control it. But I don't know why John Wayne wants to be producer, director, and star. When I'm directing, I spend all my time, day and night, concentrating on that job. For *War and Peace* I made all my time available a year in advance for story conferences. We were shooting a year. I had less time for *Solomon and Sheba*. We are born with certain talents: I don't want to act. Actors come on the set and say, 'What's he doing? I can do my job and his too.' They don't realize the director has worked and planned for months. The actor says, 'We know what we're going to do while acting and the cameraman can handle the rest.'

"I've come to the place where I don't have to go out and sell my soul for another dollar. I'm taking a stand that the picture I make will do something for people—for our country. I hope to set an example and perhaps a few others will follow."

King's mention of *War and Peace* led me to get his permission to quote extracts from some notes he made about that great picture.

NOTES FROM *WAR AND PEACE*, the film
By King Vidor

I was sitting in the California sun working on an original screenplay for an American locale when I received a telephone call from Dino De Laurentiis, the Italian film producer, asking if I would like to assume the job of bringing Leo Tolstoy's great novel *War and Peace* to the motion picture screen. I made the quickest decision I ever made in my life; there were no doubts whatever. Since my first reading of the novel all other fiction has suffered by comparison. Tolstoy reaches the depths of character, the heroic proportions, the philosophic intonations for which the peripatetic reader searches, but seldom finds.

I approached the work of transferring *War and Peace* into the medium of the cinema with humble reverence, with fidelity, and serious dedication to the task…A great work of art in literature such as *War and Peace* can be compared in strength with the power of a great symphony and similarly will not build in progressive strength if told only in a succession of unrelated culled fragments. This then was the task that lay before me in bringing *War and Peace* to the screen and instigated a search for a pattern of unity which would hold the many episodes, characters, incidents, and themes together into a thoroughly integrated scenario. Tolstoy had written a wonderful screenplay when he wrote the book…I decided to adopt the same form used by Tolstoy for the movie adaptation. On a blank piece of paper I drew three vertical lines; one on the left side, one down the center of the page, and one on the right side of the page. The first line represented Pierre's story, the second Andrey's story, and the third, Nicholas'. These vertical lines did not run concurrently; instead, each succeeding line began opposite the point where the previous line ended. At the end of the third line, I went back to line number one because I found that in his chapter headings Tolstoy had returned again to Pierre's story. As the book progressed these three stories began to converge and intermingle and their separate dramatic characteristics began to impinge, the one upon the other.

In the second half of the book and the film the pattern is supplied by the movement of the French army toward and away from Moscow. Combating Napoleon's ambitions and aggressive drive is the wise and patient General Kutusov. These two contrasting lines now dominate the entire form of the film. Our three original lines, or themes, Pierre-Andrey-Nicholas, while still running, would become secondary to the stronger motivation of the two major themes, Napoleon-Kutusov; just as in any war, our lives go in oblique directions and their normal patterns are thrown out of shape by the demands and impositions of the conflict.

For the grand denouement and climax of the entire structure all these themes must be brought together and dramatically ended. Here again Tolstoy had pointed the way which we used in the film.

As for Natasha, she permeated the entire structure as the archetype of womankind which she so thoroughly represents. If I were forced to reduce the whole story of *War and Peace* to some basically simple statement, I would say that it is a story of the maturing of Natasha. She represents to me the anima of the story and hovers over it like immortality itself.

I have never before the production of the film, or since, been able to consider any other English speaking actress available to us who could give the exact mood, grace, emotion, and perception of the character of Natasha as could Audrey Hepburn…

To what source does a maker of movies turn after drinking from the infinite and valuable fountain of Leo Tolstoy's genius?

No doubt the answers lie in the enlightenment of the progressive contemporary thoughts of our own day.

As an answer to my question about the function of the motion picture director, I chose the following paragraph from King Vidor's own autobiography.

> A director must have some familiarity with every art and craft that goes into the making of a film. He must be to some extent an actor, a writer, a scene designer, a photographer, a musician, an editor, a technician, and a painter. He must never be in the position of being completely dependent on some other fellow's decision or judgment. There must be, for best results, one conception of the entire film. A basic explanation of many poor films is that the project, though usually started with the best of intentions and integrity, simply gets diluted along the way.

CHAPTER 28

As I write this, the name William Wyler is so closely associated with the award-winning *Ben-Hur* that his previous pictures have been temporarily overshadowed; but if you think a moment, I'm sure you'll recall such directorial greats as *The Best Years of Our Lives*, *Wuthering Heights*, and many more.

I believe that the outstanding accomplishment in the direction of *Ben-Hur* was Wyler's extraordinary success in making every moment and every character of the Lew Wallace classic come alive. The film seemed to reflect problems that could be ours. To effect this in a story of ancient times was, to me, a superlative achievement.

The following letter from William Wyler speaks for itself.

> Dear Frank:
>
> I have just returned from abroad to find your letter of October 6th, hence the reason for not answering sooner. I'm at a loss to know just how to fill your request. My thoughts on the subject could fill a book too, and I don't quite know how to condense it. Anyway, it's probably too late now and that will let me off the hook. In any case, I'll be looking forward to seeing the book with much interest.
>
> Meanwhile, all good wishes for the New York and best regards.
>
> Willy

Fred Zinnemann, another Academy Award winner, wrote me from the Hotel Hassler in Rome. I mention this because I've imagined that being far away was the reason some of my colleagues didn't answer me. Naturally none of them needed an excuse. Directors are enormously busy; and what George Stevens and William Wyler wrote me could serve for the rest. It is only because I—and you too, I hope—have enjoyed reading the letters I've quoted that I'm sorry a few were unable or unwilling to talk about their work.

As the only Z on my list, Fred Zinnemann has the closing spot, and, aside from his enormous talent, it couldn't happen to a nicer guy. Retiring, modest, and wise, I'm sure his fellow craftsmen will agree that he is one of the most beloved members of his profession. Here's his letter.

> Dear Frank:
>
> Please forgive the delay. Your letter reached me here a couple of days ago and I hastened to answer.
>
> It's difficult to write a paragraph on so general a subject as directing, without being superficial or pompous, or both. I have tried to come up with something, and perhaps the following may be of some use to you. It goes without saying, that you may use it in any way you see fit.
>
> "Directing motion pictures is creative work. As a means of self-expression it is comparable to other media: writing, painting, composing music. Unfortunately, there is one important difference: the raw materials for the making of movies are infinitely more expensive (story, actors, technicians, sets, film, and so on).
>
> "Hence, the economic motive is often quite overpowering. Many considerations—in one form or another—are almost always present from the very instant of conception. In the face of this ulterior motive it is most difficult to preserve the purity and impact of the original idea, without compromise or adulteration. In most of the other creative media, the artist or craftsman, need concentrate on nothing but the struggle with his material."
>
> Dear Frank, I'm afraid it's the best I can do. It probably stinks, but at least it comes from the heart.
>
> As to the picture I most enjoyed making; it is probably a draw between *High Noon* and *The Nun's Story*.

The very best wishes for a great success for your book. I wish you could tell me more about it, if you have the inclination.

Yours always,
Fred Z.

What a beautiful letter!

Well, there you have it. A group of directors has given a variety of answers to the question about their function. And what do I think?

Before I give you one more answer to that, it might be wise to summarize briefly what the studios expect from us. That varies slightly. For instance, the director is sometimes given a completed script a few days before shooting starts; but more frequently he works with the writer during the screenplay's construction. Sometimes he makes tests and is in on the casting with the producer and the casting director. Usually he's in close touch with the set designer so that his settings are arranged in such a manner that the close shots will be as effective as the full shots. We all have different approaches to set design. In my case I take one general point of view as the key angle and eliminate one of the set's four walls entirely. I do this to simplify the set's geography for the viewers, so that the progress of an actor from left to right will not be confused by reversing the angle. However, I do use a small segment of the fourth wall to back up a reverse close up. In the case of exterior locations, the director has to know what the position of the sun will be during the day. The least interesting angle on exteriors is the one with the sun directly behind the camera, because this flattens everything. Cameramen prefer the sun to be where it will back light the actors to give them dimension.

Rehearsals are another problem. Usually the director reads the script, which is followed by a discussion of the characters. Sometimes he can rehearse in the actual sets, but a good deal of the rehearsing is done during the shooting, since the expense of carrying actors for rehearsals frequently seems unnecessary to the front office. In this case, most directors run through all the action that takes place in an episode without breaking it up into separate shots. This familiarizes the actors, the cameraman, and the crew with a rough idea of the movement of the sequence. When the actual shooting begins, it is now possible to take all the long shots first with just a few additional feet for cutting purposes.

This is done because the lighting will be considerably changed for the medium and close shots, and moving back and forth would mean a continual relight job.

I have spoken about discussing characterizations before the shooting starts. I would add that once the character is agreed upon, the director becomes more of an audience than a teller-what-to-do to the majority of actors. A few directors do constantly correct and criticize. I disagree with this practice, because I believe it inhibits and irritates any actor who knows his business. I even go so far as to watch the first rehearsals without comment so that the actors can feel their way and arrive at movements and ways of reading their lines which seem comfortable and real to them. I make corrections only when the rehearsal seems contrary to what I think the scene demands. I've never forgotten what Napoleon is reputed to have said when someone asked him how he planned the strategy of a battle. He smiled and said, "I engage my troops and see what happens." The best actors like a certain amount of freedom and a sense of creating from their understanding of the character. I believe this self-reliance should be encouraged.

What is the director's prime function? I must go back to Shakespeare's insistence on holding the mirror up to nature and his advice to Laertes to be true to himself. Dedication to the truth is to me the most important contribution a director can make to bring life to a motion picture. If he is his own boss, as so few directors are, his devotion to truth will inspire everything he does, from the choice of his story to the editing and final preview. If he has to take orders from someone else, he will still endow every moment of the film which he does control with the same determination to photograph and record what is true. Not easy—but what is that's worth a damn; and I agree with George Bernard Shaw who said, "This is the true joy in life, the being used for a purpose recognized by yourself as a mighty one, the being thoroughly worn out before you are thrown on the scrap heap, the being a force of nature instead of a feverish selfish little clod of ailments and grievances complaining that the world will not devote itself to making you happy."

Before I am thrown on Mr. Shaw's scrap heap, I should like to direct a picture about our fight for survival in the midst of the constant threat of war. Surely, the audience for such a film is infinite.

I believe this picture should be without apparent preachment and without pulling any punches; and its creators would have to approach and solve their story with such inspired devotion and skill that it would be a mighty shout to destroy today's common enemy, the killer bombs and missiles which we ourselves created—the killer bombs and missiles which can otherwise write for all of us the final

FADE OUT.

THE FILMS OF FRANK TUTTLE

Chronological Listing by Release Dates

The Kentuckians. Famous Players-Lasky/Paramount Pictures, February 20, 1921. Scenarist

The Conquest of Canaan. Famous Players-Lasky/Paramount Pictures, August 21, 1921. Scenarist

The Cradle Buster. Patuwa Pictures/American Releasing Corp., March 19, 1922. Producer, Director, Scenarist, Story-Writer

Second Fiddle. Film Guild/W.W. Hodkinson Corp., January 7, 1923. Director, Story-Writer (with James Ashmore Creelman)

Youthful Cheaters. Film Guild/W.W. Hodkinson Corp., May 6, 1923. Director

Puritan Passions. Film Guild/W.W. Hodkinson Corp., September 2, 1923. Director

Grit. Film Guild/W.W. Hodkinson Corp., January 7, 1924. Director

Peter Stuyvesant. Chronicles of America Picture Corp. (No release date known), 1924. Director

Manhandled. Famous Players-Lasky/Paramount Pictures, August 4, 1924 (copyright July 22, 1924). Scenarist

Her Love Story. Famous Players-Lasky/Paramount Pictures, October 6, 1924. Scenarist

Dangerous Money. Famous Players-Lasky/Paramount Pictures, October 20, 1924. Director

Manhattan. Famous Players-Lasky/Paramount Pictures, November 10, 1924. Writer

Miss Bluebeard. Famous Players-Lasky/Paramount Pictures, January 26, 1925. Director

A Kiss in the Dark. Famous Players-Lasky/Paramount Pictures, April 6, 1925. Director

The Manicure Girl. Famous Players-Lasky/Paramount Pictures, July 6, 1925. Director

Lucky Devil. Famous Players-Lasky/Paramount Pictures, July 13, 1925. Director

Lovers in Quarantine. Famous Players-Lasky/Paramount Pictures, October 12, 1925. Director

The American Venus. Famous Players-Lasky/Paramount Pictures, January 25, 1926. Director

The Untamed Lady. Famous Players-Lasky/Paramount Pictures, March 22, 1926. Director

Kid Boots. Famous Players-Lasky/Paramount Pictures, October 4, 1926. Director

Love 'Em and Leave 'Em. Famous Players-Lasky/Paramount Pictures, December 6, 1926. Director

Blind Alleys. Famous Players-Lasky Corp./Paramount Pictures, March 12, 1927 (New York premiere, February 26, 1927). Director

Time to Love. Paramount Famous Lasky Corp., June 18, 1927. Director

One Woman to Another. Paramount Famous Lasky Corp., September 17, 1927. Director

The Spotlight. Paramount Famous Lasky Corp., November 19, 1927. Director

Love and Learn. Paramount Famous Lasky Corp., January 14, 1928. Director

Something Always Happens. Paramount Famous Lasky Corp., March 24, 1928. Director, Writer

Easy Come, Easy Go. Paramount Famous Lasky Corp., April 21, 1928. Director

Varsity. Paramount Famous Lasky Corp., October 27, 1928. Director

His Private Life. Paramount Famous Lasky Corp., November 17, 1928. Director

Marquis Preferred. Paramount Famous Lasky Corp., February 2, 1929. Director

The Canary Murder Case. Paramount Famous Lasky Corp., February 16, 1929. Director (scenes for the "talkie" version)

The Studio Murder Mystery. Paramount Famous Lasky Corp., June 1, 1929. Director

The Greene Murder Case. Paramount Famous Lasky Corp., August 31, 1929. Director

Sweetie. Paramount Famous Lasky Corp., November 2, 1929. Director

Only the Brave. Paramount Famous Lasky Corp., March 8, 1930. Director

Men Are Like That. Paramount Famous Lasky Corp., March 22, 1930. Director

The Benson Murder Case. Paramount Famous Lasky Corp., April 12, 1930. Director

Paramount on Parade. Paramount Famous Lasky Corp., April 19, 1930. Segment Director

True to the Navy. Paramount-Publix Corp., May 31, 1930. Director

Love Among the Millionaires. Paramount-Publix Corp., July 19, 1930. Director

Her Wedding Night. Paramount-Publix Corp., September 18, 1930. Director

No Limit. Paramount Publix Corp., January 24, 1931. Director

It Pays to Advertise. Paramount Publix Corp., February 28, 1931. Director

Dude Ranch. Paramount Public Corp., May 16, 1931. Director

This Is the Night. Paramount Publix Corp., April 8, 1932. Director

This Reckless Age. Paramount Publix Corp., January 9, 1932. Director, Adapter

The Big Broadcast. Paramount Publix Corp., October 14, 1932. Director.

Dangerously Yours. Fox Film Co., January 29, 1933. Director

Pleasure Cruise. Fox Film Corp., March 24, 1933. Director

Roman Scandals. Howard Productions, Inc./United Artists Corp., December 29, 1933 (Los Angeles premiere, November 27, 1933). Director

Springtime for Henry. Jesse L. Lansky Productions/Fox Film Corp., May 25, 1934. Director, Writer, Lyric-Writer (for "Black Black Sheep")

Ladies Should Listen. Paramount Prouctions, Inc., August 3, 1934. Director

Here Is My Heart. Paramount Productions, Inc., December 28, 1934. Director

All the King's Horses. Paramount Productions, Inc., February 22, 1935. Director, Writer

The Glass Key. Paramount Productions, Inc., May 31, 1935. Director

Two for Tonight. Paramount Productions, Inc., September 13, 1935. Director

College Holiday. Paramount Pictures, Inc., December 25, 1936. Director

Waikiki Wedding. Paramount Pictures, Inc., March 26, 1937. Director

Doctor Rhythm. Major Pictures Corp./Paramount Pictures, Inc., May 6, 1938. Director

Paris Honeymoon. Paramount Pictures, Inc., January 27, 1939. Director

I Stole a Million. Universal Pictures Co., July 21, 1939. Director

Charlie McCarthy, Detective. Universal Pictures Co., December 22, 1939. Producer, Director

This Gun for Hire. Paramount Pictures, Inc., New York premiere, May 13, 1942. Director, Contributing Writer

Lucky Jordan. Paramount Pictures, Inc., week of January 25, 1943 (copyright February 26, 1943). Director

Hostages. Paramount Pictures, Inc., week beginning October 11, 1943 (copyright August 5, 1943). Director

Star Spangled Rhythm. Paramount Pictures, Inc., December 2, 1943. Contributing Director

The Hour Before the Dawn. Paramount Pictures, Inc., week of May 10, 1944 (copyright March 24, 1944). Director

Rainbow Island. Paramount Pictures, Inc., New York premiere, October 25, 1944. Director (withdrew due to illness)

The Great John L. Bing Crosby Productions, Inc./United Artists Corp., May 25, 1945. Director

Don Juan Quilligan. Twentieth Century-Fox Film Corp., June, 1945 (copyright June 13, 1945). Director

Suspense. Monogram Productions, Inc./A King Bros. Production, June 15, 1946. Director

Swell Guy. Universal-International Pictures Company, Inc., New York premiere, week of January 26, 1947. Director

Time Running Out. United Artists Corp., October 31, 1950. Director.

The Magic Face. Columbia Pictures, September 29, 1951. Director

Hell on Frisco Bay. Warner Brothers, December 22, 1955. Director

A Cry in the Night. Warner Brothers, August 14, 1956. Director

Island of Lost Women. Warner Brothers, April 3, 1959. Director

TELEVISION

Committed. General Electric Theatre, December 5, 1954. Director

Farewell to Kennedy. General Electric Theatre, November 14, 1955. Director

Crusader. CBS Primetime, 1955-1956. Episode Director

Claire. Screen Directors Playhouse, April 26, 1956. Director

UNPUBLISHED STORIES AND ESSAYS

"Blind Man's Buff"

"Cleopatra and the Cobra"

"Double Identity" (with George Julian Sinclair)

"The Fairest of the Fair"

"The Glorious Fool"

"Introduction" to Ballet Carnival (1939)

"Lady in Distress"

"My Heart Is Dancing" (1937)

"Sugar and Spice"

UNPUBLISHED SCENARIOS AND TREATMENTS

The American (with John Sherry)

Babes in Hollywood (1936)

Baby

Carmen (with John Bright)

Drop Dead

The Gang's All Here

The Gay Sextette

Honolulu Holiday (with Ralph Cedar, 1941)

Jail Break-In! (with David Robel)

A Killer at Large (1931)

A Kiss for Cinderella (with Henrietta Boehm)

Knickerbocker Holiday

Love's a Luxury (with Tatiana Tuttle)

Made in Heaven (with Viola Brothers Shore, 1936)

Mancuffed (with David Davidson)

The Manikin (with Bryce Carelton)

Mission to Israel (with George Julian Sinclair)

Pardon My Glove

Serpent's Tooth (with George Julian Sinclair)

Slap Happy

Spitin' Image (with Robert Meltzer)

Tangier Tornado

Thief in the Night

Tom Sawyer, Detective (with George Julian Sinclair)

UNPUBLISHED PLAYS

Bet Your Life (1940)

The Boys are Marching (with Irvin Thomas, 1936)

The Floor of Heaven (with Allan Gruener)

Free As a Bird (with Tatiana Tuttle)

Free As a Bird (with George Julian Sinclair)

Keep it Clean

The Merry Ha Ha

Out of Sight (1920)

The Queen's Lover

Red Cap

Red Diamond (1931)

Tales of Fatima: Time to Kill (1949)

Tinseltown Café

UNPUBLISHED SCREENPLAYS AND ADAPTATIONS

The Apple Tree (1931)

Falling Star

Head Over Heels (with Walter Brooke)

How to Know Women (with John Bright)

Pardon My Millions (with George Julian Sinclair)

The Road Back (revisions, 1939)

Temple of the Tigers (with Allan Gruener and Jo Swerling)

Until Tomorrow (with Viola Brothers Shore)

Yankee Doodle Dan (with Bryce Carelton)

WRITING ON THE DANCE

Cleopatra and the Cobra

by

Frank Tuttle

Legend had it that Leon Bakst had taken one look at Flore Revalles and instantly decided that she would be spectacularly seductive in the costumes he had designed for "Scheherazade," "Tamar," and "Cléopâtre." Bakst had shrewdly argued that the fact that Mlle. Revalles was a Swiss opera singer without any previous experience as a dancer was unimportant because what these roles called for were stage presence, the ability to move excitingly, and personal allure; and Flore Revalles possessed all these qualities abundantly.

When the Diaghilev Ballet arrived in New York in 1916, I was the assistant to the director of publicity, Edward L. Bernays. This was my second job after leaving college. The first had been as the assistant editor of *Vanity Fair*, where I had met Mr. Bernays, who had just begun the career that later developed into his extravagant success as a big time public relations councilor. The Diaghilev Ballets Russes had got off to a bad start because neither Nijinsky nor Karsavina had arrived for the opening performances and the star-conscious American public had felt cheated. When Nijinsky finally arrived, the box office zoomed upward, and his new ballet, "Til Eulenspiegel," with settings and costumes by Robert Edmond Jones, was a superlative success; but before he got here it was obvious that something radical was needed to needle the public's apathy.

1916 was the era when Walter Kingsley, who directed publicity for the Palace Theatre, had declared that a press agent was a buccaneer on the high seas of journalism; and he had himself pirated space in the journals of the day with such theatrical maneuvers as the capture of a deer in the wilds of Central Park. The deer, of course, was the cherished pet of an East Indian dancer who happened to be headlining at the Palace that week. It was this kind of hoked-up press agentry that inspired my idea for Cleopatra and the cobra. However, I was somewhat fearful that its circusy aroma might prove a trifle pungent for the sponsor of the Ballets Russes, the Ago (Otto) Kahn. But Edward L. Bernays backed me up when I timidly suggested the plot and gave me carte blanche to go ahead with the project.

The idea was simply to persuade Mlle. Revalles to be photographed in her Cleopatra costume at the Bronx Zoo with a live and (supposedly) venomous snake and then to write a story to the effect that she was studying the movements of the reptile to improve her undulations in the role of the Serpent of the Nile. Obviously the first step necessary to accomplish the scheme was to get Mlle. Revalles to agree. I hurried to the Century Theatre, where a rehearsal of "Scheherazade" was in progress. As I slid into a seat next to Mlle. Revalles' maid, who spoke English, she was smiling. She said, "Mr. Piatin just told *fonny* joke—only *fonny* in Russian."

"I know how it is," I said gratefully. Since my connection with the Ballet, I had suffered from translators who possessed a bulldog determination to translate the untranslatable. "Which one is Mr. Piatin?" I asked. The maid gestured. "The man Madame is lying on," she said. I reacted and thought of a "fonny" answer but suppressed it in the interest of promoting my plot.

During the next break in rehearsal, using the maid as interpreter, I succeeded in talking Flore Revalles into making the expedition. It developed that a friend of hers had a limousine, and we arranged to meet in front of the Reptile House the following Sunday.

My next move was to the Zoo to make all the necessary arrangements with Mr. Snyder, the curator of reptiles. Snyder was a mild, quiet man in his early forties, taciturn but cooperative. When I had outlined the plan, he suggested that we use a gopher snake for the experiment because its appearance and marking were similar to those of a cobra except that it was hoodless and that, he pointed out, was no objection since a cobra distended its head only when it was about to strike. "And," he added, "if it's supposed to be the lady's pet, it wouldn't do that—naturally."

I have the usual aversion to snakes, and our stroll through the overheated, stifling snake house produced a minor tremor in my viscera. I still remember with considerable revulsion one glassed-in enclosure where smallish snakes of assorted colors, predominantly pink, were pretzelled together in true lovers' knots and dripped profusely from the branches of a small tree that had been constructed for their convenience. There were four snakes behind the glass front to which Mr. Snyder guided me. Two of them were king snakes and the other two were the gophers. They were all asleep. One of the candidates for the job of immortalizing Mlle. Revalles was about ten feet long, the other about six. I agreed that they were imposingly sinister, and we decided to leave the final choice to Cleopatra herself.

On the way back to Snyder's office my stomach was still uneasy. I was seized with a sudden professional fear. Suppose Cleopatra backed down at the last moment. I confided my fear to the curator. Would it be possible, I asked, for him to hold the snake if Mlle. Revalles balked at the idea? "Sure," he said. "Why not? But I'll tell you something. People are funny about snakes. Sometimes they aren't bothered too much. She might even get interested. Let's just wait and see." I agreed and thanked him. "The main thing to remember about snakes," he went on, "is that they don't like you or dislike you. They just don't give a damn." We concluded the interview in the office with a few comments by Mr. Snyder on the various types of people who visited the Zoo. He told me that in the spring, at mating time, there was always an added element which came to observe the love life of their four-footed friends, and not from scientific motives. "You'd be surprised," he said, "at the number of respectable looking citizens who sit in front of the bear cage with peep-holes torn in their newspapers." I thanked him again for his kindness and took the subway back to town.

Sunday was cloudless, warm, and a pay day at the Park, which meant that the Zoo was not overcrowded. Cleopatra arrived on schedule in her friend's limousine. The friend was a middle-aged lady who spoke with a French accent. The photographer and I escorted the ladies to Mr. Snyder's office, where he had arranged for Flore Revalles to change into her Cleopatra costume. "So if someone will get it," he said, "we'll step outside till you're ready." The friend translated this. Mlle. Revalles held up her tiny handbag. "Voici," she said, and we left the office. Mr. Snyder's daughter, a bright-eyed child of ten, joined us. A few moments later Cleopatra made her entrance, and we escorted her to the glass enclosure. Snyder indicated the gopher snakes and asked her to choose one. She smiled and pointed at the ten-footer. Mr. Snyder went around to the rear of the enclosure and stepped inside. I had visualized his doing something with a forked stick, but he merely reached down and picked up the reptile, which twisted around his arm and writhed forward with deliberate unconcern, occasionally flicking its tongue. Mr. Snyder joined us and said to Mlle. Revalles' friend, "Tell her not to hold it too hard. It keeps on the move all the time. When it sticks out its neck too far, just reach out and grab it with the other hand. And whatever you do, don't drop it," he said directly to Flore Revalles. "We'd have a hell of a time getting it back."

I was watching Cleopatra. Her eyes were glistening. She had the snake away from Mr. Snyder before he finished talking. The reptile slithered across the dancer's bare and beautiful back. Her eyes dilated. She breathed ecstatically, "*Ah, c'est délicieux.*"

We wandered into the Park and found a rock where Cleopatra could drape herself. The photographer went to work. He took about twenty pictures. They were all wonderful. I remember one pose in particular. The snake slithered through Cleopatra's grip toward her face, the tongue flicking in and out as he came closer. When the flat, evil-looking head was a few inches from Flore Revalles' mouth, the graflex clicked. Cleopatra moved her face to the right. The serpent glided by her left cheek and slid across her neck.

A few minutes later we started back to the Reptile House. Snyder's little girl took the snake from Flore Revalles as though it were her skipping rope. The reptile kept on moving in its indifferent, bored way. Mlle. Revalles asked if it would be possible to buy the snake. She wanted it as a pet. Mr. Snyder said he was sorry, but that it belonged to the city. While Mlle. Revalles was changing I had a chance to study the snake at close range and found myself intrigued by the intricate texture of its skin. Mr. Snyder's daughter held it out to me and I took it. By that time it had warmed up considerably from its contact with Cleopatra's back. I was astonished to find that my instinctive revulsion had vanished and that I was simply fascinated. When Mr. Snyder returned it to the glass enclosure I was almost sorry to let it go.

The picture and the story were a mild sensation. They appeared in the press of America from coast-to-coast. And today, when I am confronted with a snake either in captivity or in its natural habitat, I am filled with precisely the same loathing that was mine before my adventure with Cleopatra and the snake.

INDEX

Adler, Larry, ii, iv
Adler, Luther, 153–154
Allen, Gracie, 86, 87, 109
Allied Artists, 142
All the King's Horses, 101, 204
The American Venus, 47, 48, 58, 202
Anderson, Richard, 171–172
André, Michael, 149–150, 152
The Apple Tree, iv, 101, 213
Apron Strings, 24, 25, 26. See also *The Cradle Buster*
Arnold, Edward, 94, 102, 103, 105
Arthur, Jean, 69, 71
Astor, Mary, 23, 27, 54
Auer, Mischa, iii, 88

Bakst, Léon, 11, 215
Ball, Lucille, 94
Barbier, George, 99, 110, 111
Barnes, Binnie, 130
Basch, Greta, 154, 155, 156
Baxter, Warner, 88
Belita, 142–146
Benchley, Robert, 9
Bendix, William ("Bill"), 134, 135, 137, 138
Ben-Hur, 195
Bennett, Joan, 106
Benny, Jack, 109
The Benson Murder Case, 73, 203
Bergen, Edgar, 115–116
Berkeley, Busby, 93

Bernays, Edward L., 11, 12, 215, 216
The Big Broadcast, 86, 87, 88, 204
Binney, Faire, 13
Blondell, Joan, 137, 138
Blue, Ben, 109
Blue, Monte, 14
Boehm, Carla, ii
Boehm, Henrietta, 209
Boehm, Sidney, 163
Boland, Mary, 106, 109
Bolton, Guy, 88, 89
Borgnine, Ernest, 167
Bow, Clara, 27, 29, 43, 53, 54, 73, 82
Bren, Milton, 115, 161, 162
Brent, Evelyn, 56, 57, 58, 59
Brian, Mary, 73
Brisson, Carl, 101–102
Britton, Barbara, 139, 141
Broken Arrow, 179, 180
Brooks, Louise, 47, 48, 56, 58, 64, 65
Bullitt, William Christian ("Bill"), 23
Burns, Bob, 110, 111
Burns, George, 86, 87, 109
Burr, Raymond, 171, 172

Calloway, Cab, 86, 87
The Canary Murder Case, 64, 65, 203
Cantor, Eddie, 14, 53, 54, 91, 92, 93, 95, 96
Capra, Frank, 112, 123, 172, 173, 174, 178
Carlisle, Kitty, 99, 100

Carroll, Nancy, 71, 72
Carroll, Sue, iii, 121, 122, 163
Carver, Tina, 156, 171
Ceder, Ralph, 94, 96
Chaplin, Charlie, 35, 48, 112
Charlie McCarthy, Detective, 115–116, 205
"Claire," 169, 206
Clark, Dane, 147, 148, 149, 151, 152
Coffee House Club, 9, 12, 18, 24
Cohan, George M., 4
Cohen, Manny, 101
College Holiday, 109, 110, 111, 204
Comedy Club, 16, 19, 54
The Conquest of Canaan, 20, 21, 201
Cooper, Gary, 72, 73
Corrigan, Lloyd, 71, 127
Courtot, Marguerite, 26
The Cradle Buster, 24, 26, 201
Creelman, James Ashmore ("Jim"), 24, 27, 31, 63, 201
Cregar, Laird, 118, 119, 120
Cromwell, John, 69, 107, 175
Cronyn, Hume, 125
Crosby, Harry L. ("Bing"), 79, 86, 87, 99, 100, 106, 110, 111, 112, 113, 114, 138, 139, 205
Crowninshield, Frank, 9, 12, 111
Crusader, 169, 206
A Cry in the Night, 171, 172, 205
Cukor, George, 177, 178

Damita, Lili, 85, 86
Dangerously Yours, 88, 204
Dangerous Money, 38, 39, 49, 202
Daniels, Bebe, 38, 39, 41, 45
Darnell, Linda, 140, 141
Daves, Delmer, 178–180
de Cordova, Arturo, 134, 135, 136
Demarest, William, 163, 164
DeMille, Cecil B., ii, 73, 109
DeMille, Katherine, 55, 73
DeSylva, Buddy, 117, 118, 121
Devine, Andy, 112, 113
Diaghilev Ballets Russes, 11, 12, 215, 216

Disney, Walt, 161
Dix, Richard, 20, 38, 46, 63
Dodds, Josephine, 4, 5, 6
Don Juan Quilligan, 137, 138, 205
Donlevy, Brian, 105, 171, 172
Dortort, David, 171
Dozier, William, 117, 128
Dru, Joanne, 163, 164
Dude Ranch, 80, 204
Duke, Robert, 149, 150, 151
Dwan, Allan, 31, 32, 33, 34, 35, 50

Easton, Jean, 32, 33, 35
Edwards, Blake, 161–162, 163, 168
Eldridge, Florence, 66, 69, 71, 88
Ellington, Duke, iv
Ellis, Mary, 101
Erickson, Leif, 109, 110
Errol, Leon, 188
Erwin, Stuart ("Stu"), 72, 79, 80, 86

Fairbanks, Douglas, Sr., 19, 31, 66
Farley, Morgan, 69
Ferrer, José, 180, 181
Film Guild, vi, 24, 27, 31, 37, 38, 56, 63, 86, 87, 201
Fontanne, Lynn, 45–46
Foote, Sterling, 16
Foran, Dick, 115
Ford, Harrison, 45
Ford, John, 107
Free As a Bird, iv, 211
The Frontier of the Stars, 13

Gaal, Franciska, 113–114
Gallagher, Skeets, 83, 84
Galsworthy, John, iv, 101
Geraghty, Tom, 19, 20, 21, 31
The Glass Key, 102, 103, 105, 110, 121, 204
Glazer, Barney, 85, 86, 87, 88
Goldwyn, Samuel, 91, 92, 93, 94, 95, 96, 97
Gordine, Sasha, 147, 148, 152
Gould, Harold, 16
Grant, Cary, 85, 86, 99

Index   221

Grant, James Edward ("Jimmy"), 139, 140, 141
Gravet, Fernand, 148, 149, 150, 151
Gray, Johnny, 63
Gray, Larry, 47, 48, 53, 56
The Great John L., 139, 141, 205
The Greene Murder Case, 69, 203
Green, Mitzi, 82-83
Griffith, David Wark, 21, 66, 159, 160
Griffith, Raymond ("Ray"), 35, 41, 43, 61, 62, 79, 94, 121
Grit, 27, 29, 201

Hamilton, Neil, 66, 125
Hammett, Dashiell, 102, 103, 105, 147
Hathaway, Henry, 67
Head, Edith, 29, 72, 136–137
Hell on Frisco Bay, 163, 164, 205
Here Is My Heart, 99, 100, 109, 204
Hervey, Irene, 171, 172
Her Wedding Night, 43, 79, 203
Hill School, 4, 72, 182
Homolka, Oscar, 135
Hopper, Hedda, 63–64, 189
Hornblow, Arthur, Jr., 91, 92, 93, 110
Horton, Edward Everett, 99, 114
Hostages, 133,134, 135, 136, 205
The Hour Before the Dawn, 128, 129, 130, 131, 205
House Committee on Un-American Activities, i
Hunt, J. Roy, 38, 39, 46, 47
Hunt, Marsha, 109
Hunter, Glenn, 24, 27, 31

Indrisano, John ("Johnny"), 141
International Film Union, 154
Intolerance, 19
I Stole a Million, 115, 205
It Pays to Advertise, 83, 84, 204

Jacobs, Lewis, 159, 160, 161
Jones, Billy, 80–81
Jory, Victor, 115

Kane, Helen, 72
Kane, Henry ("Hank"), 147, 148, 152
Kaufman, George, 31, 91
Kazan, Elia, 182
Keep It Clean, 55
Keith, Brian, 169
Kent, Sidney, 31–32
The Kentuckians, 14, 19, 20, 21, 201
Kenyon, Doris, 21
Kid Boots, 53, 54, 55, 91, 202
King Brothers (Frank and Maurice), 142, 146
King, Stoddard, 15
A Kiss in the Dark, 49, 50, 202
Kober, Arthur, 137, 138
Kohlmar, Fred ("Freddy"), 94, 127
Koster, Henry ("Bobby"), 182–183
Kramer, Stanley, 185
Kruger, Otto, 140, 141
Kubrick, Stanley, 186

La Cava, Gregory, 46, 88
Ladd, Alan, iii, 105, 118, 121, 122, 127, 162, 163, 164, 169, 171, 187
Ladies Should Listen, 99, 204
Lake, Veronica, iii, 118, 119, 120, 121, 128, 129, 130–131
Lang, Charles ("Charlie"), 112–113
Lansbury, Angela, 169
Lasky, Jesse, 37, 38, 57, 201–203
Lauder, Sir Harry, 73
Leacock, Stephen, 9
LeBaron. William, 34, 46, 101, 137, 138
Lee, Dixie, 79
Leifels, Felix, 12, 13
Leonard, Sheldon, 127, 128
Lillie, Beatrice ("Bea"), 112, 113
Lloyd, Harold, 39
Lombard, Carole, 47, 83, 84
Love Among the Millionaires, 82, 203
Love 'Em and Leave 'Em, 56, 58, 59, 202
Lovers in Quarantine, 45, 46, 202
Lucky Devil, 46, 202
Lucky Jordan, 127, 205

Lunt, Alfred, 45–46

McCarey, Leo, 91, 139
McCarthy, Charlie, 115–116
McClure, Gregg, 139–140
MacDonald, Dwight, 166, 167
McDonald, Marie, 127, 128
MacKenna, Kenneth, 43, 49
MacLeish, Archibald ("Archie"), 135
McLeod, Norman, 188
The Magic Face, 153, 154, 205
Maigne, Charles, 13, 14, 21, 25
The Male Animal, 123, 125, 140
Maltz, Albert, 117
Mamoulian, Rouben, 107
Manhandled, 31, 32, 35, 37, 201
The Manicure Girl, 45, 202
March, Fredric ("Freddy"), 66, 73, 74, 75
Marion, George, Jr., 62, 71, 72, 85, 86, 87
Marshall, George, 186–187
Martin, Townsend, 24, 27, 38, 42, 47, 49, 50, 53, 56
Maugham, Somerset, 128, 129, 130
Meighan, Thomas, 13, 20, 21, 22, 58
Meiklejohn, Bill, 121, 123
Menjou, Adolphe, 48, 49, 63, 94
Merz, Charles Andrew ("Doc"), 15, 50
Myerson, Robert ("Bob"), 155, 156
Milestone, Lewis, 41, 107
Miss Bluebeard, 41, 43, 49, 202
Montgomery, George, 169
Moore, Douglas Stuart, 16
Moore, Tom, 34, 39, 40
Moore, Victor, 45
Mowbray, Alan, 94
My Man Godfrey, 47, 84, 88

Nazimova, Alla, 13
Neill, Roy, 21, 22
New York Philharmonic Orchestra, 12
Nijinsky, 11, 12, 215
No Limit, 29, 79, 203
Nugent, Elliott, 123, 125

Oakie, Jack, 71–72, 80, 83
O'Brien, Edmond, 171, 172
Oland, Warner, 66
Oliver, Edna May, 46, 47, 48
Only the Brave, 72, 73, 203

Pahlen, Victor, 147, 148, 149, 152
Paige, Mabel, 127
Paiva, Nestor, 163
Pallette, Eugene ("Gene"), 66, 69, 73, 80, 84, 101, 142, 143, 144, 145
Paramount Pictures, iii, 8, 13, 14, 19, 20, 21, 22, 23, 24, 25, 26, 31, 32, 34, 35, 37, 38, 41, 43, 45, 47, 50, 53, 56, 57, 64, 65, 66, 69, 82, 83, 84, 86, 87, 88, 94, 99, 101, 105, 109, 110, 113, 114, 117, 121, 123, 125, 128, 133, 136, 137, 163, 201–205
Paris Honeymoon, 113, 204
Parker, Dorothy, 9
Patuwa Pictures, 24, 201
Paxinou, Katina, 134, 135
Perkins, Osgood, 24, 25, 27, 31, 56, 57, 59
Peter Gunn, 162, 168
Petit Raymond, 152
Pleasure Cruise, 88, 89, 204
Porter, Edwin S., 159–160
Powell, William ("Bill"), 8, 39, 40, 47, 51, 62, 64, 69, 73
Preston, Robert ("Bob"), iii, 118, 119, 120
Pringle, Aileen, 49, 50, 63, 84

Quentin Durward, iv, 15, 16
Quinn, Anthony ("Tony"), 55, 110, 111

Rackin, Martin ("Marty"), 163
Raft, George, 102, 103, 105, 115
Rainer, Luise, 134, 135, 136
Rainger, Ralph, 85, 87, 99, 110, 111
Ralston, Esther, 46, 47, 48, 57, 63, 66
Raye, Martha, 109, 110, 111
Revalles, Flore, vi, 11, 12, 215, 216, 217, 218
Revere, Anne, 137, 138

The Rise of the American Film, 159, 160
Robin, Leo, 87, 99, 110, 111
Robinson, Edward G., 69, 163–164
Rockett, Al, 88
Rodakiewicz, Henwar, 106, 110
Rogers, Charles ("Buddy"), 63
Roman Scandals, i, 14, 91, 92, 94, 95, 96, 204
Ross, Shirley, 110, 111, 114,
Ruggles, Charlie, 43, 79, 85, 86

Saint Bartholomew's Eve, iv, 16
St. Clair, Malcolm ("Mal"), 57, 63, 64
The Scarecrow, 27. See also *Puritan Passions*
Schulberg, Ben, 84
Screen Directors' Guild, 107, 173, 175
Second Fiddle, 27, 201
Seitz, John, 76, 88, 121
Semenoff, Simon, 141
Sennett, Mack, 35, 41, 63, 87, 94, 161
Shakespeare, William, iv, 55, 165, 166, 198
Shaw, George Bernard, iv, 19, 37, 44, 198
Sheikman, Arthur, 92, 94
Sheldon, Lloyd, 31, 37, 38, 49, 53
Shuftan, Eugene ("Gene"), 151
Siegel, Sol, 8, 133, 136
Signoret, Simone, 148, 149, 150, 151, 152
Silvers, Phil, 137, 138
Smirnova, Tatiana ("Tania"), ii, 124, 209, 211
Smith, Henry Clapp, 16
Smith, Kate, 86, 87
Smith, Stanley, 71
Staats, Fredericka, ii, 6, 20
Stanislavski, Constantine, 27, 166
Steinway, Theodore, 16
Sterling, Ford, 47, 48
Stevens, George, 20, 41, 123, 133, 187–188, 196
Stewart, James ("Jimmy"), 180, 183, 186
Stewart, Paul, 163, 164
Strong, Austin, 16, 18, 19, 20, 43, 66
Stroheim, Erich von, 21

Struss, Karl, 111, 142
The Studio Murder Mystery, 66, 67, 203
Stuart, Gloria, 94, 106
Sullivan, Barry, 142, 143
Suspense, 142, 143, 146, 205
Sutton, John, 130, 131
Swanson, Gloria, 32, 33, 34, 35, 49, 50
Sweetie, 70, 71, 203
Swell Guy, 144, 205
Swerling, Jo, 112, 213

Tamiroff, Akim, 99, 114
Taurog, Norman, 188–189
This Gun for Hire, i, 117, 118, 122, 123, 205
This Is the Night, 85, 86, 204
Thompson, Harlan, 100, 109, 113
Thompson, L. Keene, 72, 73, 74
Time to Love, 61, 63, 94, 202
Time Running Out, 147, 151, 205
Tobin, Genevieve, 88, 89
Todd, Thelma, 85, 106
Tone, Franchot, 128, 129, 130
Treen, Mary, 137
Trevor, Claire, 115, 162
True to the Navy, 73, 74, 75, 79, 203
Turnbull, Hector, 65, 66
Tuttle, Barbara (daughter), ii, 2, 124
Tuttle, Elizabeth ("Bess") (sister), 4, 5, 6, 8
Tuttle, Fred Bradley (father), 3, 4, 5, 6, 7, 8, 25, 37, 38
Tuttle, Fredrika (daughter), ii, iv n., 6, 17, 28, 96
Tuttle, Helen Hislop Dodds (mother), 3, 4, 5, 6, 7, 8
Tuttle (Votichenko), Helen (daughter), ii, iii, iv, vi, 2, 28, 96, 123
Twentieth Century-Fox, 137, 180, 188, 205
Two for Tonight, 106, 204

Universal Pictures, 115, 205

Van Dine, S.S. (Willard Huntington Wright), 64, 69, 105

Vanity Fair, 9, 10, 13, 16, 111, 172, 215
Vidor, Florence, 63, 112
Vidor, King, 107, 112, 167, 189, 190, 191, 193
The Village, iv, 19

Waikiki Wedding, 110, 111, 121, 204
Walker, Helen, 127, 128
Waller, Fred, Jr., 24, 25, 26, 27, 31, 87
Wanger, Walter, 13, 14
War and Peace, 190, 191–193
Warner Brothers, 64, 69, 94, 137, 163, 164, 171, 205
Wellman, William, 107
Whiting, Richard, 71
Wiman, Dwight Deere, 24, 26, 31, 85
Winters, Shelley, 125
Wodehouse, P.G., 9, 88
Wood, Natalie, 171, 172
Woolley, Monty, 15, 16, 23
Wray, Fay, 163
Wright, Stanton MacDonald, 104, 105, 106
Wyler, William, 123, 133, 195, 196

Yale University Dramatic Association, 15, 16, 24
Yordan, Philip ("Phil"), 142
Young, Roland, 55, 85, 86, 88, 89, 99
Youthful Cheaters, 27, 201

Zanuck, Darryl, 88, 137, 138, 180
Ziegfeld, Florenz ("Flo"), 48, 53, 92
Zinnemann, Fred, 195, 196–197
Zukor, Adolph, 109, 110, 112

BearManorMedia

P O Box 750 * Boalsburg, PA 16827

Hollywood's Golden Age
by Edward Dmytryk
$17.95   ISBN: 0-9714570-4-2

A legend remembers the good old days of films…Edward Dmytryk, director of The Caine Mutiny, Murder, My Sweet, Hitler's Children and a host of other classic movies, has written a powerful memoir of his early days in Hollywood. From peeking in at the special effects for The Ten Commandmants, the original silent film, to his first job as an editor, slowly, patiently splicing film…Dmytryk's brilliantly written and until now unpublished look back on old Hollywood is a joy you won't be able to put down.

My Fifteen Minutes
An Autobiography of a Warner Brothers Child Star
by Sybil Jason $18.95   1-59393-023-2

Sybil Jason was Warner Brothers' first child star. Friend of Humphrey Bogart, Roddy McDowall, Freddie Bartholomew, Shirley Temple and dozens of other Hollywood stars, her fan club is still international. Her captivating story is enriched with over 100 rare photos from her personal collection.

A Funny Thing Happened on the Way to the Honeymooners…I Had a Life
by Jane Kean
$17.95   ISBN: 0-9714570-9-3

Jane Kean's frank and funny memoirs of a show business life are a loving first-hand account of what it was like growing up among the Who's Who of classic Hollywood and Broadway. She tells all—and tells it like it was. From starring stage roles in *Early to Bed*, *Call Me Mister*, and *Ankles Aweigh*, to such presitigious films as Disney's *Pete's Dragon*, Ms. Kean has lived the show biz life. Having performed extensively with her comical sister Betty, Jane is perhaps best known as Trixie in the award-winning television series, *The Honeymooners*.

visit www.bearmanormedia.com
Visa & Mastercard accepted. Add $2 postage per book.

BearManorMedia
P O Box 750 * Boalsburg, PA 16827

Plain Beautiful:
The Life of Peggy Ann Garner

The life story of one of Hollywood's most beloved child actors, whose performance in *A Tree Grows in Brooklyn* won her the Oscar.

$19.95   ISBN 1-59393-017-8

Spotlights & Shadows
The Albert Salmi Story

You know the face. You know the credit list: *Lost in Space, Escape from the Planet of the Apes, Gunsmoke, Bonanza, Kung Fu, The Twilight Zone* and hundreds more…But who was Albert Salmi?

Sandra Grabman's biography is a frank and loving tribute, combined with many memories from Salmi's family, friends, and co-stars, and includes never-before-published memoirs from the man himself. From humble beginnings—to a highly successful acting career—to a tragic death that shocked the world—Albert Salmi's story is unlike any other you'll ever read.

$19.95   ISBN: 1-59393-001-1

visit www.bearmanormedia.com
Visa & Mastercard accepted. Add $2 postage per book.

CHECK THESE TITLES! BearManorMedia.com

P O Box 750 * Boalsburg, PA 16827

Comic Strips and Comic Books of Radio's Golden Age
by Ron Lackmann

From Archie Andrews to Tom Mix, all radio characters and programs that ever stemmed from a comic book or comic strip in radio's golden age are collected here, for the first time, in an easy-to-read, A through Z book by Ron Lackmann!

$19.95   ISBN 1-59393-021-6

Perverse, Adverse and Rottenverse
by June Foray

June Foray, voice of Rocky the Flying Squirrel and Natasha on Rocky and Bullwinkle, has assembled a hilarious collection of humorous essays aimed at knocking the hats off conventions and conventional sayings. Her highly literate work is reminiscent of John Lennon, S.J. Pearlman, with a smattering of P.G. Wodehouse's love of language. This is the first book from the voice of Warner Brothers' Grandma (Tweety cartoons) and Stan Freberg's favorite gal!

$14.95   ISBN 1-59393-020-8

The Old-Time Radio Trivia Book
by Mel Simons

Test your OTR knowledge with the ultimate radio trivia book, compiled by long-time radio personality & interviewer, Mel Simons. The book is liberally illustrated with photos of radio stars from the author's personal collection.

$14.95   ISBN 1-59393-022-4

The Writings of Paul Frees

A full-length screenplay (The Demon from Dimension X!), TV treatments and songs written for Spike Jones—never before published rarities. First 500 copies come with a free CD of unreleased Frees goodies!

$19.95   ISBN 1-59393-011-9

How Underdog Was Born
by creators Buck Biggers & Chet Stover

The creators of Total Television, the brains behind Underdog, Tennessee Tuxedo and many classic cartoons, reveal the origin of one of cartoon's greatest champions—Underdog! From conception to worldwide megahit, the entire story of the birth of Total Television at last closes an important gap in animated television history.

$19.95   ISBN 1-59393-025-9

Daws Butler – Characters Actor
by Ben Ohmart and Joe Bevilacqua

The official biography of the voice of Yogi Bear, Huckleberry Hound and all things Hanna-Barbera. This first book on master voice actor Daws Butler has been assembled through personal scrapbooks, letters and intimate interviews with family and co-workers. Foreword by Daws' most famous student, Nancy Cartwright (the voice of Bart Simpson).

$24.95   ISBN 1-59393-015-1

For all these books and more, visit www.bearmanormedia.com or write info@ritzbros.com
Visa & Mastercard accepted. Add $2 postage per book.

www.ingramcontent.com/pod-product-compliance
Lightning Source LLC
Chambersburg PA
CBHW031311150426
43191CB00005B/182